Interpreting Mathematical Economics and Econometrics

Interpreting Mathematical Economics and Econometrics

Byron D. Eastman
Laurentian University

St. Martin's Press   New York

ISBN 0-312-42477-9
ISBN 0-312-42478-7 (pbk.)

Library of Congress Cataloging in Publication Data

Eastman, Byron.
  Interpreting mathematical economics and econometrics.

  1. Economics, Mathematical.   2. Econometrics.
3. Economics - Mathematical models. I. Title.
HB135.E27   1984   330′.028   84-8303
ISBN 0-312-42477-9
ISBN 0-312-42478-7 (pbk.)

Contents

Preface

This book is written for those who fear mathematics. If you often say, 'I was never very good at maths', but now have to confront aspects of the subject, this book is for you. The title has been chosen carefully. The operative word is **interpreting**. The complex mathematical and statistical techniques which are used to arrive at sophisticated results are ignored. Only the results are important. But even these are usually presented in an esoteric, jargon-laden fashion. Fortunately, the interpretation of these results is straightforward. Unfortunately, the textbooks which are the usual route to such an interpretative understanding assume a substantial amount of mathematical training. When confronted with page upon page of matrix algebra, most of the lower case and half of the upper case of the Greek alphabet, all but the most dedicated students decide that they 'didn't really need that course anyway'. The lay person who wishes to be informed about the details of the results of some recent research will be quickly turned away by the existence of 'econometric estimations', and discussions of 'regression coefficients', 'standard errors', and so on. But such is the stuff of research — mathematical/statistical jargon is pervasive. The ideas represented by the jargon are simple. There is no good reason for the use of Greek letters, except 'by convention'. If someone were to simply interpret and explain 'in plain English' the meaning of the jargon and of the mathematical and statistical (Greek) symbols, the difficulty would disappear. This book provides such an interpretation.

The encroachment of mathematics into many social

vii

sciences has been accelerated by the computer. Computers have enabled more and more sophisticated analyses to be done by less and less sophisticated computer users. The advent of the 'personal' or 'home' computer is further amplifying this effect. An increasing number of people are undertaking complicated analyses using the 'packaged' computer programs available on all ranges of computers without the ability to fully interpret the results of their work. These 'packages', or, as they are called in the jargon of the computer industry, 'software', are themselves getting more sophisticated enabling the most naive of computer users to undertake the most complicated of statistical analyses. The missing link is the ability to interpret these results. Part II of this book provides that link.

This book came to be written because of an expressed need by many generations of students for a non-technical, non-mathematical, non-statistical introduction to the meaning of mathematical symbolism and econometric analyses.

My motivation has been to enable those with no training in calculus or statistics to understand the results of the applications of these powerful tools. This is the book I searched for in vain when first confronted with the terrifying requirement that I must understand the meaning of 'partial differentials' and 'partial regression coefficients'. There is no pretence of rigour in the presentation of the mathematics. Stress is placed on the understanding of the results of research from an intuitive viewpoint.

The book is divided into two major parts. The first, consisting of Chapters 1 to 4, deals with the tools of the differential and integral calculus. Chapter 1 introduces mathematical notation for the most extreme form of novice and builds on that foundation in Chapter 2 as the use of equations is explained. Chapters 3 and 4 discuss the meaning of the principal results of differentiation and integration.

Part II addresses econometric analyses. Chapter 5 bridges the gap from the theoretical modelling to the statistical testing of those models. Included in Chapter 6 is a discussion of the most important statistics associated with econometric analyses. These form the actual 'testing' of a theory. Chapter 7 discusses the most serious problems which can arise in regression analyses.

The context of the book is economics but the applications are general. Anywhere that mathematics is used or statistical analyses are required the same interpretations are valid. Parts of the book have been used to assist students undertaking research in such varied fields as economics, psychology, sociology, political science, history, chemistry, biology, physics, business studies and physical education.

BYRON D. EASTMAN

ACKNOWLEDGEMENTS

The author and publishers wish to thank the following who have kindly given permission for the use of copyright material.

Biometrika Trustees for a table from *Biometrika*, Volume 38 (1951) by J. Durbin and G. S. Watson.

Iowa State University Press for a table from *Statistical Methods*, Seventh Edition, by George W. Snedecor and William G. Cochran © 1980.

Macmillan Published Company Inc. for Table IV from *Statistical Methods for Research Workers*, 14th Edition, by the late Sir Ronald A. Fisher. Copyright © 1970 by the University of Adelaide.

*To Rachel, Alexander and Timothy for helping
me to interpret what's important*

PART I

MATHEMATICAL ECONOMICS

1

Mathematical Symbolism

Introduction

The first thing we must do is introduce some basic mathematical concepts. I am going to assume you have no mathematical background. The first thing a mathematical economist does is replace words with symbols so that price may become p, quantity may become Q, and so on. Of course, the symbol used is completely arbitrary: price could be represented by Y and quantity by X, for example. Most writing, however, prefers to relate the symbols in some way to the words they represent. The words represented and the symbols used are referred to as **parameters** and **variables**.

Variables

Mathematical symbolism may refer to constants or variables. A constant is a quantity which takes a fixed value in a specific problem. The constant may be presented as a number or a symbol denoting a number in which case it is called a **numerical** or **absolute** constant. Alternatively, the constant may be presented as a symbol and is called an **arbitrary** or **parametric** constant, usually abbreviated simply to parameter. Absolute constants take on the same value in all situations whereas parameters, while assuming only one value in a specific problem, may take different values in other problems. Parameters are most frequently represented by letters at the beginning of the alphabet, although there are sufficient exceptions not to make this a definitional rule. Some writers prefer the Greek alphabet with the parameters represented by its first letters, $\alpha, \beta, \gamma, \delta$, etc.

Table 1.1 presents the Greek alphabet. Familiarity with it should remove the anxiety resulting from the esoteric quality surrounding its use.

Variables can be thought of as quantities which assume a variety of values in a specific problem. (The set of possible values is called the range of the variable.) Commonly, pure mathematics uses the letters at the end of the alphabet, for example, X, Y, Z, to represent variables but in applied mathematics this convention is sometimes broken; the symbol used is often simply the first letter of the variable name, for example, p represents the variable price, q represents quantity, and so on.

Variables may be classified in many ways. One classification scheme dichotimises variables as either continuous or discrete. **Continuous variables** can take values within a specified interval of real numbers. Because **any** value in the interval can be taken, and because these values can differ by infinitely small amounts, it is not possible to count all the values in, say, the interval between 1 and 10. Put another way, there are no gaps in a continuous variable over the range between 1 and 10. **Discrete** (discontinuous) **variables**, on the other hand, **are** countable and are often defined as being able to take only

Table 1.1 *The Greek alphabet and English couterparts*

Greek		English		Common usage
Capital	Small			
A	α	alpha	A a	constant
B	β	beta	B b	constant
Γ	γ	gamma	C c	constant
Δ	δ	delta	D d	special operator: increments
E	ϵ	epsilon	E e	variable
Z	ζ	zeta	Z z	variable
H	η	eta	Y y	variable
Θ	θ	theta	– –	functional operator
I	ι	iota	I i	parameter
K	κ	kappa	K k	parameter
Λ	λ	lambda	L l	parameter
M	μ	mu	M m	parameter
N	ν	nu	N n	parameter
Ξ	ξ	xi	X x	variable
O	o	omicron	O o	–
Π	π	pi	P p	Π: special constant
P	ρ	rho	R r	variable
Σ	σ	sigma	S s	summation operator
T	τ	tau	T t	variable
Υ	υ	upsilon	U u	variable
Φ	ϕ	phi	F f	functional operator
X	χ	chi	– –	statistic
Ψ	ψ	psi	G g	functional operator
Ω	ω	omega	W w	variable

values which are specified in a **countable** range. In other words, discrete variables do have gaps. An example of a discrete variable is the price of a commodity if the price is given only in pennies. The price, say p, is then a discrete variable which assumes values which are a set of integers – a range which is discontinuous.

Another popular classification scheme divides variables into four categories: independent, dependent, exogenous and endogenous. **Independent** variables are those that do not depend on other variables. Now, it is important to distinguish between the mathematical and economic concepts of dependence. Dependence in the purely mathematical sense does not require **causality**. The mathematics only establishes a rule for

associating the two variables; a systematic relationship is
suggested but there is no information about **why** the variables
move together. We do not know whether X influences Y, or
Y influences X, whether some external factor makes X and Y
move together, or whether it is by pure chance that X and Y
move together. All that can be said is that if we know the
value of one variable we can find the value of another.

Dependence in the economic context is not arbitrary.
Economists usually try to write what they think is the
dependent variable as the one that is being changed by
the **independent** variable -- the independent variables cause
the change. For example, if we say that an increase in the
price of a pizza causes fewer pizzas to be demanded each
week then we are saying that the quantity of pizza demanded
depends on the price. Quantity is therefore a dependent
variable and price is an independent variable. Price is an
independent variable because we have not said anything
affects it. Notice that if we said that price depends on something else, we would make pizza price a dependent variable
and something else would be independent. It is all a matter of
what affects what. If our hypothesis is simply that price
affects quantity demanded **and we stop there** then quantity
demanded is a dependent variable and price is independent.

Exogenous and **endogenous** variable classifications refer to
the broader context of a complete model but are related in
some ways to the dependent–independent dichotomy. An
exogenous variable is the easiest one to define because it is
placed so as to depend on nothing in the model. Nothing
affects it as far as we are concerned. It is something which is
taken as given in our economic model – values for it come
from outside the model. Some writers use the term **autono-
mous** or **predetermined** rather than exogenous. If the quantity
of pizza demanded depends not only on price but also on,
say, the population of a city, and we have no interest in
explaining what determines the population of a city, then the
population variable is exogenous. It is **outside** ('ex') the scope
of what we want to explain and we treat it merely as given in
our model of what determines the quantity of pizza demanded.

An endogenous variable is, like a dependent variable, one
which is dependent on others. In the pizza example, quantity

demanded is an endogenous variable because it depends on such things as the price of the pizza and the population of the city. Hence, **if a variable is dependent then it is also endogenous.** But if a variable is endogenous, it is not necessarily dependent. To illustrate, we will expand our discussion a little about how much pizza is sold by adding one more variable, the price of wheat. We suggested that the quantity of pizza demanded is determined by the price of the pizza and population. Now, let us add that the price of the pizza is affected by the price of wheat. We now have pizza price **affecting** quantity demanded and being **affected by** wheat price. Pizza price is therefore an independent variable when we say it **affects** quantity and a dependent variable when we say it is **affected by** wheat price. Whether we consider pizza price dependent or independent depends entirely on which part of the model is being referenced.

But with the endogenous–exogenous split, the answer is more clear cut. The first hypothesis has quantity demanded depending on pizza price and population. The second hypothesis has pizza price depending on wheat price. The total model therefore has two exogenous variables (they depend on nothing within our model) – population and wheat price are exogenous because our hypotheses do not try to explain how they are determined.

The dependent–independent split only comes into play when we consider each hypothesis **separately.** Hypothesis one (that quantity of pizza demanded is dependent on pizza price and population) has quantity demanded as dependent and pizza price and population as independent **in that hypothesis.** Hypothesis two (that pizza price depends on wheat price) has pizza price as dependent and wheat price as independent **in that hypothesis.**

The dependent–independent split relates to each hypothesis **separately**; the endogenous–exogenous split relates to all the hypotheses together, i.e. the 'model'.

We see then that variables can be dependent, independent, endogenous or exogenous and often more than one of these at the same time. But how are variables related mathematically? That is, how are the verbal hypotheses put into mathematical hypotheses? The answer is through equations.

2

Equations

Verbal hypotheses into mathematical functions

An equation is the mathematical method of relating variables. The verbal economic hypotheses of the last section can be accurately represented by equations. The most general form an equation can take is represented by the mathematical shorthand for 'Y is a function of X':

$$Y = f(X) \tag{2.1}$$

The word 'function' simply means 'is determined by', so here Y 'is determined by' X. This merely says that Y is mathematically dependent upon X. Given a value of X, we can find the value of Y; that is, we have a rule for obtaining the value of Y when we are given the value of X.

But note that some of the conventional rules of algebra are

not being observed in our functional notation. The statement $Y = f(X)$ does **not** mean 'Y equals f times X', the parentheses do not mean multiplication as they would in elementary algebra. Rather, the 'f' represents the rule by which X is transformed into Y – it tells us what must be done to the X to get the Y. Often, the rule is applied to only certain values of the variables. If we are not interested in the negative prices of pizza or the negative quantities demanded then we would restrict the rule relating these two variables to positive values only – the rule is said to be **defined** for positive prices and quantities only.

This is related to what we mean when we speak of the **domain** of the function. The domain of the function $Y = f(X)$ is the interval of values **for** X over which the function is defined. When we restrict $f(X)$ in a similar fashion (say to positive values only) we are defining the **range** of the function, i.e. the values which Y can take, **given our rule**.

This is a convenient point to introduce the ideas associated with **explicit** and **implicit** functions. The statement that $Y = f(X)$ is called an explicit function; Y is an explicit function of X because there is a definite rule specifying how the value of Y is determined by the value (arbitrarily) chosen for X. Similarly, because we have seen that mathematical dependence implies nothing about economic dependence or causation, we could say that X is a function of Y. This is another explicit function, this time with the values of X being determined by the rule operating on the values of Y that are chosen.

Now, if we feel that the values of X and Y are connected or related in some special way (i.e. that they are not independent of one another) we may write them in the **implicit** form as

$$f(X, Y) = 0 \qquad\qquad (2.2)$$

The implicit function states

(1) That there is a mutual relationship between the X and the Y variables.
(2) That each variable determines the other.

The explicit functions corresponding to this implicit function are called the **inverses** of each other. (It should be noted that not all functions have inverses.)

In this book we shall concentrate on the class of functions known as single-valued functions. Single-valued functions permit only one value of Y to correspond with each value of X. This is opposed to multi-valued functions which may have more than one value of Y corresponding to each value of X.

Many of these ideas can be clarified through mathematising the hypotheses of the last chapter. We first have to define symbols for the variables. Let Q_D be the quantity of pizza demanded, P_P be the price of pizza, P_W be the price of wheat, and N be population. Then the first hypothesis – quantity of pizza demanded depends on the price of pizza and population – can be written as the explicit function:

$$Q_D = f(P_P, N) \tag{2.3}$$

Here we are saying that the quantity demanded is a function of the price of pizza and population, i.e. quantity **depends on** price and population. Notice how the functional notation accommodates more than one independent variable. The convention is simply to place the independent variables inside the brackets and separate them by commas.

The second hypothesis can be written:

$$P_P = g(P_W) \tag{2.4}$$

That is, the price of pizza is a function of (depends on) the price of wheat.

Perhaps this is an opportune place to reintroduce the difference between the purely mathematical and economic interpretations of the dependent/independent variable relationship. Let equation (2.4) illustrate the analysis. We have two variables which, mathematically, 'determine' each other. In implicit form, the function may be written:

$$G(P_W, P_P) = 0 \tag{2.5}$$

Now, the explicit form we have chosen is with P_P dependent and P_W independent. Mathematically, the point of view we have chosen is completely arbitrary. The function *per se* is not a causal relationship; P_W does not **cause** P_P. **Causes and effects occur between actual phenomena, not between measures of the variables.** A function interpreting the causes and the effects, as equation (2.2) does, simply concentrates on the view of the function with P_P dependent and suppresses the inverse. This is the effect of the economics. From a purely mathematical point of view, both explicit functions may be of equal interest.

The first hypothesis (equation (2.3)) represents a model of the determination of the quantity of pizza demanded. The second represents a model of the determination of pizza price. The equations (or models) can be brought together to give a bigger (and sometimes better) model of what we are trying to explain. The result is a two-equation model:

$$Q_D = f(P_P, N) \tag{2.3}$$

$$P_P = g(P_W) \tag{2.4}$$

Using equations we can more easily define dependent, independent, endogenous and exogenous variables although the endogenous/exogenous distinction is the more important. If the complete version of our model is given by equation (2.3) alone, then Q_D is a dependent and an endogenous variable and P_P and N are independent, exogenous variables. If we bring in equation (2.4) and call the set (or 'system') of equations the model we have Q_D and P_P as dependent variables; P_P, N and P_W as independent variables; and N and P_W as exogenous variables.

As you may have noticed, whenever we felt we knew the direction of causation between our variables, we wrote the causes as the independent variables and the effects as the dependent variables. In this context we can formulate some guidelines for defining variables.

- **Rule 1.** Any variable on the left-hand side of an equals sign is automatically dependent in that equation.

- **Rule 2.** Any variable on the right-hand side of an equals sign is automatically independent in that equation.

So, dependent and independent categories apply only to **positions in equations.**

- **Rule 3.** Any variable which appears on the left-hand side of an equals sign of at least one equation in a model is an endogenous variable in that model.
- **Rule 4.** Any variable which only appears on the right-hand side of the equals sign, never on the left-hand side, of any equation in a model is an exogenous variable in that model. (This, of course, excludes 'equilibrium' conditions in equation form where, for example, 'supply' is made equal to 'demand'.)

So now, when economists (or any scientists, for that matter) throw around the variable types you will know what they are referring to – simply to the position of the variable in the model.

More about functions

We have seen that variables can be related in equation form and that they can be read as, say, 'Q is a function of P', in

$$Q = f(P) \qquad (2.6)$$

The 'f' is used to indicate the idea of a function, but there is no requirement that the letter f be used. Any letter of any alphabet of any language can be used. If more than one equation is used, then, as you have noticed, the convention is to use different letters to replace the f. Favourite letters for this type of substitution are the English 'g' and 'h', and the Greek letters ϕ ('phi') and θ ('theta'). Not worrying about the meaning of the variables, examples of various notations are:

$$Q = F(i, M) \qquad (2.7)$$

$$Q = g(i/M) \tag{2.8}$$

$$M = h(i,\ L^3) \tag{2.9}$$

$$S = \phi(D,\ P) \tag{2.10}$$

$$D = \theta(P,\ 1/r,\ 2ii/3 - V^3) \tag{2.11}$$

But, whatever notation is used, they all read, 'something is a **function of** something else'. Some authors may substitute the 'is a function of' phrase with a literal translation of the mathematical notation. For example, equation (2.7) may be read 'Q equals f of i and M'; equation (2.8), 'Q equals g of i/M'; and so on.

One other notation which has some popularity replaces the 'f' with the dependent variable as in:

$$I = I(i) \tag{2.12}$$

$$C = C(Q) \tag{2.13}$$

Again, there is no multiplication of I times i or of C times Q implied.

This is still read 'I is a function of i' and 'C is a function of Q'. However, by far the most popular letter to express the concept 'is a function of' is the letter 'f'.

Equations (2.7) and (2.8) permit the introduction of a distinction between variables and **arguments**. So far, we have referred to variables but excluded any discussion of arguments. Mathematics puts a very specific definition on the concept of an argument. This is best understood through examining the functions presented in equations (2.7) and (2.8). In both, Q is a function of two variables, i and M. However, in (2.7), i and M are given as separate determinants of Q (they are separated by a comma in the parentheses). This means that the f is a rule under which values for i and M are put individually – each pair of numbers for i and M affect Q. Here, the i and the M are the **arguments** of the function.

In equation (2.8), although both i and M appear as independent variables, it is their **ratio** which affects Q. Hence, if they both change in such a way that the ratio does not change, there is no change in Q. The ratio, i/M is the **argument** of this function.

Now, the functions we have been using have been expressed in general notation. We have not specified what is called the 'functional form'. The analytical form which a function takes provides us with a means of grouping 'types' of functions. The distinction between functional forms is best indicated through the use of examples.

The general functional form may be written, as we have done:

$$C = C(Y) \tag{2.14}$$

However, the function may be specified as

$$C = 25 + 0.75Y \tag{2.15}$$

and this can be rewritten

$$C = a + bY \tag{2.16}$$

where: $a = 25$, and $b = 0.75$.

Equation (2.16) is the **linear functional form**. From a purely mathematical point of view (i.e. ignoring the economic theory), the parameters, a and b can be any numbers. The a is called the **intercept** of the C axis and the b is the **slope** of the function. Figure 2.1 illustrates the analysis. If $a = 25$, the distance $cd = 75$, the distance $ef = 100$, we have a slope of $cd/ef = 75/100 = 0.75$. This gives us the equation presented above:

$$C = 25 + 0.75Y \tag{2.15}$$

The linear functional form is extremely popular in economics largely because a solution can always be found (assuming one exists) in linear models whereas for nonlinear models this is not always true. Further, even where observed economic behaviour suggests nonlinear functional forms, it is possible to usefully employ linear techniques. Two popular methods are

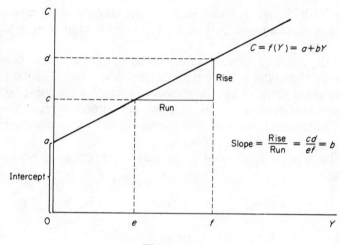

Figure 2.1

(1) Transforming a nonlinear model into a linear one,
(2) Approximating a curve with a straight line.

A simple example of a transformation is given by the function:

$$Z = aX^b \tag{2.17}$$

Taking logarithms of both sides of the equation, we obtain

$$\log Z = \log a + b \log X \tag{2.18}$$

which is a function linear in the log of the variables.

Where such transformations are not possible the frequent practice is to make an approximating assumption that the functional form is linear within a (small) neighbourhood of the point in which we are interested. This is often what is done when a straight line is constructed tangent to a curve at some specified point. Consider the suggestion that the functional relationship between consumption (C) and income (Y) is nonlinear and we are interested in the relationship between C and Y at some point, say R in Figure 2.2.

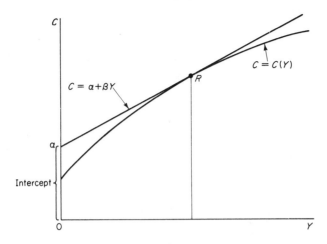

Figure 2.2

We can approximate the relationship between C and Y with a tangent to $C(Y)$ at R. The equation for the tangent is a straight line and, in a small neighbourhood around R, it is suggested to approximate $C(Y)$.

We have seen how mathematical economists formulate their thoughts in a symbolic notation. But they go further than simple formulation – they manipulate their equations, advancing hypotheses more specific than previously possible. After the variables have been defined and related in the manner discussed the usual first step is to examine the relationships using the tools of the differential and the integral calculus.

3

The Differential Calculus

The derivative

Calculus is concerned with rates of change and as such, its primary interest is in **variables** as opposed to **constants**. Suppose, for example, it is observed that an increase in the amount of money spent on advertising results in an increase in the sales of a firm. The hypothesis is that advertising increases sales, or, symbolically, sales is a function of advertising:

$$\text{SALES} = f(\text{ADVERTISING}) \qquad (3.1)$$

The variable **sales** (S) 'depends' on the variable **advertising** (A). Altering advertising will bring about some change in sales. Now, let us say that expenditure on advertising (A) changes by some small amount. The small amount is conventionally written with the letter d before the symbol representing the variable. The *d* therefore means nothing more than a very small part of the variable to which it applies. A small amount of *A* is written *dA* and is called a **differential of** *A*. Calculus is based on this idea of a small bit of a variable – a differential of the variable.

If *A* changes in size by *dA*, its magnitude becomes *A+dA*. But notice that if advertising expenditures change then sales will also change. The resulting change in sales (*S*) can be written as a differential as well – *dS*. So sales takes on the value *S+dS*. Although there is a remote possibility that *dA* may be the same size as *dS* it will most likely be different and we will assume that to be the case. That is, *dA* will be of a different size than *dS*. (However, this does not mean that *dS* will necessarily move in the same direction as *dA*.)

Figure 3.1 illustrates a possible relationship between Advertising expenditures (*A*) and Sales (*S*).

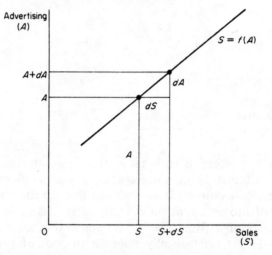

Figure 3.1

When the level of expenditure on advertising is *A*, the level of sales is *S*. The function relating advertising to sales is upward sloping indicating a **direct** relationship so that an increase in advertising will cause an increase in sales. When advertising increases from *A* to *A+dA*, sales grows to *S+dS*. If advertising expenditure increased by $1000.00 and sales rose by $5000.00 we would say that each dollar of the increase in advertising expenditure generated five dollars in increased sales. In Figure 3.1, the $1000.00 increase in advertising expenditure would be represented by the dA and the $5000.00 increase in sales would be the dS. The ratio of dS to dA may be written

$$\frac{dS}{dA}$$

This ratio, usually read 'dS by dA' or 'the differential of S with respect to A', is the most sought after entity in the differential calculus. If we keep in mind that the many complicated analyses using calculus can be reduced to the search for this simple ratio, much of the difficulty of interpreting calculus can be removed. It was a ratio like this which was examined by the two inventors of the calculus, Sir Isaac Newton and G. W. Leibniz, but there were differences in jargon. They referred to variables which changed as ones which 'flowed' and the differential itself was not called by that name but rather referred to as the 'fluxion' of the quantity in question.

The example we used has looked at the relationship between two variables, A and S. The **process** of finding the relationship between changes in these variables, dS/dA (the differential of S with respect to A), is called **differentiating**. But there is an important qualification necessary. In the advertising–sales example used above, the size of the dA was $1000.00 and the size of the dS was $5000.00. These are not particularly small numbers. But the definition of the 'd' in the derivative is supposed to be very small. The dA is supposed to be a 'little bit' of A or an 'element' of A. A common way to handle this small change in a variable is to consider the ratio dS/dA as the **change in S per unit change in A**. Interpreting the differential in this way saves a lot of difficulty in many economic applications.

Consider another example – the relationship between the quantity (Q) of output produced and sold by a firm and the amount of revenue (TR) generated by that sale. In functional notation:

$$TR = f(Q) \hspace{4cm} (3.2)$$

The differential of TR with respect to Q is

$$\frac{dTR}{dQ} \hspace{4cm} (3.3)$$

This differential describes the change in the amount of revenue going to the firm when it alters its output by one unit. In this interpretation, the differential is the familiar economic concept: marginal revenue.

Verbal analyses of the behaviour of the revenue received by firms as they vary their output usually cause no major problems for students of economics. But, introduction of calculus by way of a differential generates unnecessary anxiety. The use of **symbolism** need not cause problems if only these symbols are interpreted for what they represent – a shorthand notation for the longer verbal hypotheses. Using the differential in a statement of the form:

$$dTR/dQ=7$$

merely means that the marginal revenue of the firm at its current output level is seven. Alternately, another interpretation is that an increase in output of one unit generates an increase in revenue of seven dollars. This reveals that the units of measurement in a differential are the same as the variables which the symbols represent. If $dTR/dQ=7$, with the TR measured in dollars and the Q measured in physical units of output, the differential has a value of **seven dollars per unit**.

Another common use of the differential is in the context of **time**. Many variables change through time and when this occurs, there is frequent use of the word **rate**. The word rate itself implies a ratio. The top of the ratio refers to the occurrence of something and the bottom of the ratio refers to the length of time it takes for that event to happen. For example, suppose that we hear that the price level is rising at an 'incredible' rate. Further investigation may reveal that in the last five years the price level index has gone up 50 points. The rate of increase in the price level index (*CPI*) is 50 points per five years. But this is an awkward way to put it. The differential could be stated

$dCPI/dt$=50 points/5 years

But remember that the 'd's' are supposed to be very small. Most authors write of a 'per unit change' in the context of differentials. Therefore the $dCPI/dt$ is usually made to represent such a change. That is, rather than 50 points per five-year period we usually read of a rate of change of 10 points per year. The **rate of growth** of the price index is 10 points per year: $dCPI/dt$ = 10. The differential again refers to the rate at which one variable is changing with respect to another.

The second derivative

Every once in a while one hears the comment that we are experiencing 'accelerating inflation' or that the price of gold is rising 'faster and faster' or that the fall in share prices on the Stock Exchange is 'becoming more and more rapid'. Each of these observations and others in a similar vein refer to the idea of a differential – but not of the (first) differential as described earlier in this chapter. They are best described by the **second differential**. Consider the concept of 'accelerating inflation'. A popular journalistic phrase, this refers to the fact that inflation is increasing. If inflation refers to a change in the price level then increasing inflation must refer to an **increase in the rate of increase in the price LEVEL**. The first derivative refers to the rate of change in the price **level**. The second derivative refers to the rate of change in this rate of change. The second derivative is the **derivative of the first derivative**. If the price level is measured by some consumer price index (CPI), then inflation is represented by $dCPI/dt$. Call this inflation rate R. Then the rate of change of the inflation rate is dR/dt. That is

$$\frac{dCPI}{dt} = R \qquad (3.4)$$

and

$$\frac{dR}{dt} = A \tag{3.5}$$

therefore

$$A = \frac{dR}{dt} = \frac{d\left(\dfrac{dCPI}{dt}\right)}{dt} \tag{3.6}$$

The last equation can be interpreted as follows. An accelerating rate of inflation is the first derivative of the rate of change in the price level. The accelerating rate of inflation is a derivative of a derivative. The notation for this is $d^2 CPI/dt^2$ and is read 'd two *CPI* by dt squared'.

This second derivative is often used in economic applications to express these ideas of changes in the rate of change. If the inflation rate is increasing the mathematical interpretation would have a second derivative of a price level function with a positive number. Similarly, if the inflation were getting less and less, the second derivative would have a negative number indicating a negative rate of increase in the inflation rate. Note that this is not a decrease in the price **level** but rather a decrease in the **rate of increase** in the price level. Because there is still inflation (prices are rising) the first derivative is positive, but if the rate of increase in the rate of inflation is diminishing (prices are rising but less and less rapidly), the second derivative will be negative.

Notation

There are many ways to write the derivative. Most of these different notations are the source of great anxiety for the mathematically uninitiated. They all reduce to the same idea of a ratio of two changes. Here are some of the more common notations in use with respect to derivatives. For generality, assume a function relating a dependent variable Y to an independent variable X.

$$Y = f(X) \qquad (3.7)$$

The first derivative can be written as we have done: dY/dX. Another notation uses the idea of a 'prime' ('). In this case the first derivative is written using the 'f' from the functional notation as follows: f'. Sometimes the functional notation's 'f' is used directly: $df(X)/dX$. Lastly, especially if the derivative is taken with respect to time, many authors use a dot over the variable which is changing through time. For example, $\dot{Y}$ is equivalent to dY/dt.

Second derivatives are written in similar formats. For example, all the following are equivalent statements representing the second derivative:

$$\frac{d(dY/dX)}{dX} = f'' = \frac{d^2Y}{dX^2} = \ddot{Y} \qquad (3.8)$$

Partial differentiation

The discussion so far has concerned functions with only one independent variable. But most economic analyses are characterised as 'multivariate' because of the many variables which are suggested to influence any single economic entity. That is, there is almost always more than one independent variable.

Consider the possibility that the quantity of a product produced (Q) depends on the quantity of labour (L) and the quantity of capital (K) used in the production process:

$$Q = f(K, L) \qquad (3.9)$$

We are interested in the effect on output of changes in the quantities of labour and capital. A specific question may inquire into how output changes in response to a change in the level of employment but **with the amount of capital held**

constant. Alternately, we may want to know the effect on output of changes in the amount of capital but **with the amount of labour held constant.** The question could become more sophisticated by examining the reaction of output to changes in the amount of labour as capital moves from one level to another.

The answers to these questions are found by taking the partial derivatives of equation (3.9). The partial derivative differentiates a function of many variables with respect to only **one** of them while keeping the other variables constant. The partial derivative of equation (3.9) with respect to L specifies how output changes when the quantity of labour changes, **given some fixed amount of capital.** It is most frequently written as follows:

$$\partial f / \partial L$$

The 'backward six' is the lower case Greek letter delta and usually designates a partial derivative. This, of course, is the familiar economic concept of the marginal product of labour. The partial derivative $\partial f / \partial K$, on the other hand, explains how output changes when the amount of capital varies **with constant labour.**

Each partial derivative illustrates how the dependent variable changes when only one independent variable changes at a time – the other variables are held constant. But at what value are they held constant? The level at which unchanging variables are held constant may have a noticeable effect on the value of the partial derivative. In fact, it is sometimes interesting to see how the relationship between one independent variable and the dependent variable changes as some other causal variable changes. For example, suppose we want to know how the relationship between the quantity of labour and output changes as more capital is added to the production process. We would first take a partial derivative of the production function, equation (3.9), with respect to labour to establish that relationship. We would then take another partial derivative of that function, but this time with respect to capital. This would appear as:

$$\frac{\partial(\partial Q/\partial L)}{\partial K}$$

The taking of a derivative first with respect to one variable and then with respect to another as we have just done is called taking **cross-partials** and the results are called **second-order cross-partials**. It may be that increasing the amount of labour from 15 to 16 adds 10 units to the output of the firm when there are five machines in the shop. But how is this altered when there are 8 or 10 or 20 machines? Would a change in employment from 15 to 16 people still add 10 units to output as the quantity of machinery grows? This is the sort of question answered by the information contained in the cross-partial.

Sometimes, it is interesting to take a partial derivative twice with respect to the same variable. That is,

$$\frac{\partial(\partial Q/\partial L)}{\partial L}$$

The information contained in this second-order derivative is interesting. The first partial reveals how output varies as labour varies. The second-order partial reveals how this relationship changes as the quantity of labour itself changes. In other words, it distinguishes the effect of changes in the amount of labour on output when there is comparatively little labour from the effect of changes in the amount of labour on output when there is a lot of labour. The second-order partial illustrates how the marginal product of labour changes as the quantity of labour changes.

The economic interpretation of partial derivatives is very informative and the preceding discussion helps to reveal why they are used so much in research. The production function specified in equation (3.9) relates output to the two inputs, labour and capital. When a partial derivative is taken with respect to each independent variable, the result has a specific economic interpretation. For example, the partial derivative of output with respect to capital outlines how output changes when capital changes. But these changes are usually visualised as very small. Again, the common interpretation is a **unit** change in the independent variable. So what we have with a partial derivative is the change in output resulting from a unit change in capital input with the amount of labour held constant. But this is the familiar economic concept of the **marginal productivity of capital**. This is the economic interpretation – the first partial of the production function with respect to capital is the marginal productivity of capital. The second partial with respect to capital illustrates how the marginal productivity of capital changes as the quantity of capital itself changes. Most analyses of production functions therefore specify the conditions for the production function as follows:

$$Q = f(K, L) \tag{3.10}$$

$$\frac{\partial f(K, L)}{\partial L}, \; \frac{\partial f(K, L)}{\partial K} > 0 \tag{3.11}$$

and

$$\frac{\partial(\partial f(K, L))}{\partial L^2}, \; \frac{\partial(\partial f(K, L))}{\partial K^2} < 0 \tag{3.12}$$

The symbol, $>$, means 'greater than' and the symbol, $<$, means 'less than'. The use of these symbols permits a compact shorthand method of specifying whether two variables are directly or inversely related. The specification of a partial derivative as being greater than zero ('>0') is merely another way of saying that it is positive. Similarly, a negative partial derivative is written as '<0'.

The first partial, for example, states that the marginal productivity of labour is positive – as more people are hired, the quantity of output increases. The second partial states that the marginal productivity of labour, although positive, is declining as more labour is added to the firm's work-force. This is the familiar proposition called the Law of Eventually Diminishing Returns. Notice that the mathematical symbolism is much more concise. Often writers will say that the production function has the 'usual properties' implying that these conditions on the first and second partials of the production function with respect to labour apply. Diagrammatically, the first partial derivative suggests that there is a positive relationship between the quantity of the inputs and the amount of output. That is, more labour means more output. Such a relationship is depicted as an upward sloping function between output and labour as in Figure 3.2.

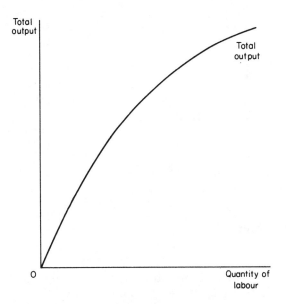

Figure 3.2

The second-order partial derivative of the production function with respect to labour is negative. That means that the amount of output increases as labour is added but **at a decreasing rate**. The increases in output resulting from each additional unit of labour get less and less – **the marginal product of labour is falling**. This is depicted indirectly in Figure 3.2 as a flattening of the slope of the production function and directly in Figure 3.3 as a negative slope relating the marginal productivity of labour to the amount of labour.

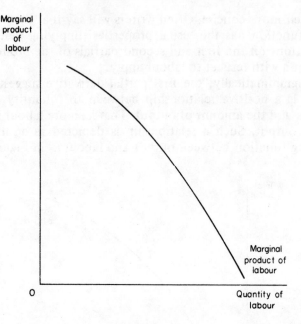

Figure 3.3

Other notation

There are several other notations for expressing partial derivatives. Unfortunately there is no consistency from author to author on the notation so it is wise to be familiar with the most common ones. Several equivalent ways to write first-order partials are:

$$\partial Y/\partial X = \partial f(X, Z)/\partial X = f_X = f_1 = f'$$

The notation on second-order partials can be even more confusing:

$$\partial(\partial f(X, Z)/\partial X)/\partial X = \partial(\partial f/\partial X)/\partial X = \partial^2 f/\partial X^2 = \partial^2 Y/\partial X^2 = \ddot{Y}$$
$$= f_{11} = f'' = f_{XX}$$

Cross-partials have many similarly confusing notations:

$$\partial(\partial f(X, Z)\partial X)/\partial Z = \partial(\partial f/\partial X)/\partial X)/\partial Z = \partial^2 f/\partial X \partial Z$$
$$= \partial^2 Y/\partial X \partial Z = f_{X,Z} = f_{12}$$

This chapter should have removed some of the anxiety associated with mathematical notation. The big hurdle is the frequent use of the Greek alphabet. Once we are over that, the differential calculus becomes less frightening. But another part of the calculus provides similar problems. It is concerned with reversing the differentiation process and is called the integral calculus.

4

The Integral Calculus

Integration

The differential as explained and interpreted in Chapter 3 takes very small changes in the variables concerned. The underlying method was to relate the rate of change in one variable to the rate of change in another. Like many other operations in mathematics, differentiation can be reversed. The reverse of differentiation is called **integration**. The objective is to find the **whole** of something when given only a 'part' of it. This 'part' has been called dy and what we want to find is Y as a function of X. Integration is the method that accomplishes this. For example, the derivative of Y when it is a function of X is

$$dY/dX = f'(X)$$

and is called the 'differential equation'. This can be rewritten

$$dY = f'(X)\,dX$$

This is called its 'differential form'. If all the little dY's are added up, we would have the 'whole' Y. But to get the desired value of Y we must add up all the values of the right-hand side of the equation. The symbol used for this 'adding up' is the sign for integration, an elongated 'S', $\int$. The differential equation, relating how a small change in the independent variable, X, causes a change in the dependent variable, Y, can be mathematically manipulated to reveal how the **level** of X is related to the **level** of Y. Using the symbol for this adding-up manipulation we get:

$$Y = \int f'dX$$

which is often written to include the variables in the function:

$$Y = \int f'(X)\,dX$$

Whereas differentiation was the process of dividing a relationship into very small parts and then observing the effect of a small change in one part or another, integration is concerned with adding up these small parts to establish the relationship between complete entities. In this sense, integration and differentiation are reverse processes. For example, the economic concept of marginal revenue specifies how total revenue changes as the quantity of output varies. Often, this relationship is derived from analysis of the total revenue function by differentiating it with respect to output:

$$dTR/dQ = f'(Q)$$

But is it possible to begin with information about the marginal revenue only and discover how total revenues vary with output? This would require reversing the differentiation process, that is, integrating the marginal revenue function. If:

$$dTR/dQ = f'(Q)$$

Then

$$TR = \int f'(Q)\,dQ$$

Figure 4.1 presents a diagrammatic analysis of the 'summing up' idea suggested by integration.

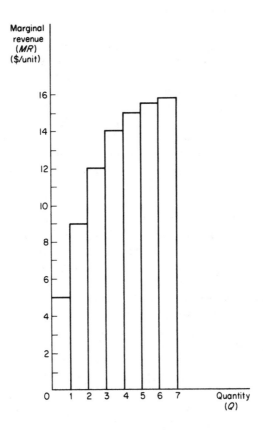

Figure 4.1

Figure 4.1 illustrates the relationship between marginal revenue and output. That is, if output rises by one unit the total revenue changes by an amount equal to the marginal revenue. But marginal revenue is the first derivative of total revenue (*TR*), so, if

$$TR = f(Q)$$

and

$$MR = dTR/dQ = f'(Q)$$

then a unit change in output causes a change in total revenue which is equal to the marginal revenue – simply the first derivative of the total revenue function. The unit change in output changes total revenue by dTR/dQ or $f'(Q)$. To obtain the total revenue corresponding to any level of output from information about the marginal revenue we simply add up all the marginal revenues until that output is reached. For example, to discover the total revenue corresponding to the output of seven units we just add the marginal revenue of the first unit (\$5.00) to the marginal revenue of the second unit (\$9.00) to the marginal revenue of the third unit (\$12.00), and so on until the seventh unit is reached. This gives us a total revenue of \$5.00 + \$9.00 + \$12.00 + \$14.00 + \$15.00 + \$15.50 + \$15.75 = \$86.25. The procedure is the same for any level of output: for three units total revenue is \$5.00 + \$9.00 + \$12.00 = \$26.00; for five units it is \$55.00, and so on.

The unit changes in quantity are of a discrete, measurable size, i.e. 'one unit'. Another way to add these up is to use a new mathematical symbol, the capital Greek letter sigma, Σ. Therefore, instead of writing:

$$TR = MR_1 + MR_2 + MR_3 + \ldots + MR_n$$

for the '*n*' units of output, we could substitute the summation notation as a sort of shorthand:

$$TR = \sum_{i=1}^{i=n} MR_i$$

which is interpreted as 'the sum of all the *MR*'s from the first one ($i=1$) to the last one in which we are interested – the

'nth' one ($i=n$)'. The total revenue for the output level of seven is \$86.25. We could use this shorthand notation to explain how this figure was obtained as follows:

$$TR = \sum_{i=1}^{n} MR_n = \$86.50$$

Now, this summation notation works fine with these comparatively large changes in output. But, what if we considered smaller and smaller changes in output (assuming the output could be divided easily into smaller and smaller pieces) until the changes in output were extremely tiny? (Mathematicians take this idea to an extreme and consider changes that are **infinitely** small.) As the changes in output get smaller and smaller, the rectangles whose areas we are adding up get smaller and smaller until there are so many of them that the marginal revenue function loses its appearance to a stairway ('a step function') and changes its shape to a continuous line. In the extreme, this continuous line represents the behaviour of marginal revenue as output changes by infinitely small amounts. As soon as we have this sort of continuous line as a representation of the relationship, the sigma, Σ, is replaced by the elongated S. That is, as the changes in the quantity of output diminish in size the formula for the addition of the marginal revenues changes from

$$\sum_{i=1}^{n} MR \text{ across the desired range of outputs}$$

to

$$\int f'(Q) \, dQ \text{ across the desired range of output}$$

All of this is really just a complicated way of finding the **area** between the marginal revenue curve and the quantity axis or as it is often called, simply, 'the area under the curve'. The Σ form of the summation represents an **approximation** to the area which the integral makes exact. The area under the marginal revenue curve between zero output and any specified output is the total revenue accruing to the firm for that output. Figures 4.2(a) and (b) illustrate the relationship between the marginal revenue and the total revenue as output changes.

The area under the marginal revenue curve grows at an increasing rate until the output of 10 is reached and then it continues to grow but at a decreasing rate. The total revenue

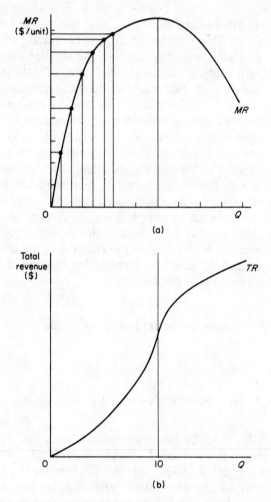

(a)

(b)

Figure 4.2

similarly grows at an increasing rate until the output of 10 is reached and thereafter increases at a diminished rate. The integral of the marginal revenue function will give us information about the value of the total revenue at any specified level of output.

Once again, the notation used in calculus (in this case, the notation used in the **integral calculus**) is awe-inspiring and certainly capable of generating high anxiety simply because of the intimidating use of mathematical notation. However, once we pass that notational hurdle, the 'adding-up' concept is a very straightforward, simple idea.

PART II

ECONOMETRICS

5

Testing Theories

Introduction

A great deal of the theorising in economics uses the techniques of the differential and integral calculus discussed in the preceding chapters. Although many theories are interesting in themselves and the mathematical processes passed through have an innate 'beauty' of their own, the purpose of a theory is to explain. The test of a theory is how well it explains. Good theories explain very well; bad theories explain poorly. The usual way to test a theory is to subject it to the available evidence and if the predictions of the theory are borne out by the data the theory is good. If the data representing the variables move in relationships that are different from those specified in the theory, the theory is rejected.

Theories are often arrived at deductively. Within the theories the magnitude of the suggested relationships are not specified, just the predicted signs on them with the result that variables are often predicted to 'vary directly', 'vary inversely', or be of uncertain sign. Estimation of the size of the relationships is the domain of **econometrics** which uses a combination of economic statistics, economic theory and mathematical economics in a unified way.

Although the origin of econometrics is difficult to pinpoint, it became prominent with the formation of the Econometric Society in 1930 which published the first issue of an important academic journal, *Econometrica*, in 1933. Econometrics was seen as the intermediary between general theoretical hypotheses and day-to-day observable facts. It permitted the 'quantification' of the qualitative theoretical relationships.

Quantifying relationships

Economic **theory** usually specifies the variables to be included in a functional relationship. Such an hypothesis is one which relates some dependent variable, Y, to a set of independent variables, $X_1, X_2, \ldots, X_n$. It could be placed in the form:

$$Y = f(X_1, X_2, X_3, \ldots, X_n) \qquad (5.1)$$

The implication of this form of equation is that the independent variables 'cause' the Y to take on the value it does. This would follow directly from the theoretical underpinnings of the model represented by this equation. These theoretical underpinnings, established on the basis of pure economic theory, are accepted and not questioned once the statistical testing of the model is begun (although they may be altered if the test turns out poor results). The economic theory is usually able to reveal the conceptual variables which should enter the model as represented by equation (5.1). Frequently, the theoretical formulation of the model is discussed at some length to outline the intricacies of the theory. In these discussions, many authors assume a numerical value specifying the magnitude of the relationship between the variables. For example, the theorist may say that the quantity (Q) of pizza eaten per month is related to the price (P) of the pizza. That is

$$Q = f(P) \hspace{3cm} (5.2)$$

Further, the theory may predict that there is an inverse relationship between the quantity of pizza demanded and the price – the lower the price, the greater the quantity of pizza demanded. But how 'big' is the relationship? That is, for every dollar decrease in the price of pizza, how many more pizza are demanded? That is the 'size' of the relationship. If, for explanatory purposes, the author of a theory suggests that a one dollar decrease in the price increases the quantity demanded by 4000, then that is the size of the relationship. The '4000' figure is a coefficient representing the size of the relationship. The relationship with the **assumed** numerical value could be written

$$Q = a - 4000P \hspace{3cm} (5.2a)$$

But if such a figure is only for explanatory purposes, what is the **real** size of the relationship? What do real world data say is the magnitude of the effect of price on quantity demanded? These latter questions are in the realm of econometrics.

This appeal to real world data is done in two contexts. Empirical observations can be gathered first in a **time-series** context. This means that the behaviour of the variables is examined **through time**. An example could apply to the demand for pizza model just discussed. Perhaps we could obtain numbers relating to the number of pizzas demanded per month from the local pizza retailers. If we could also obtain numbers describing the price of the pizza corresponding to each month we could then try to relate the quantity of pizza demanded to the price.

Time-series data would appear in tabular form (see page 46).

Table 5.1

Month	Quantity	Price
Jan.	4000	15.00
Feb.	4100	14.90
Mar.	4200	14.80
Apr.	4300	14.70
May	4400	14.60
Jun.	4500	14.50
Jul.	4600	14.40
Aug.	4700	14.30
Sept.	4800	14.20
Oct.	4900	14.10
Nov.	5000	14.00
Dec.	5100	13.90

The second context for the data is **cross-sectional**. Cross-sectional data represent **one point in time**. At any single point in time, numbers are gathered representing different members of some group such as people, firms, industries, countries, and so on. An example of a cross-sectional data set which is frequently used is a census. The census may contain data for the average wage paid in 100 occupations at the point in time at which the data was gathered. It may also reveal the average educational attainment of the workers in each occupation as well as such variables as average age, percentage of the occupational labour force that is female, and so on. All these variables are represented by data gathered at a point in time – they are cross-sectional data.

Once the theory has dictated which variables are to be included in the model and the relevant data have been gathered, whether they are time-series or cross-sectional, the task of the econometric testing is to describe, in **quantitative** terms, the relationships between the dependent variable and each independent variable. Some theories give clues about the relationships because they hypothesise the 'sign' of the relationship. That is, they specify whether direct or inverse relationships are expected. This is called a **qualitative** prediction. Although these qualitative predictions may be discussed in terms of direct or inverse variation between the relevant variables, the phrase used most frequently is: 'the sign of the partial derivative'. If direct variation is predicted, this qualitative hypothesis is 'the sign of the partial derivative is positive'. If inverse variation is expected we read 'the sign of the partial derivative is negative'.

Consider a model explaining the relationship between the rate at which crimes (C) are committed in some geographical context and a set of explanatory variables including the unemployment rate (U), average household income (Y), clearance rate for typical offences (CR), percentage of the population aged 15 to 24 (YP) and the average value of housing in the area (V). This could be specified in equation form as follows:

$$C = f(U, Y, CR, YP, V) \qquad (5.3)$$

Along with this functional form we could provide some predictions derived from the theorising which gave rise to the model. The predictions will be qualitative in nature and will suggest whether to expect direct or inverse variation between individual sets of dependent and independent variables. These are often written as partial derivatives and would usually appear immediately below the equation representing the model. The partial derivative is written as the derivative of the dependent variable with respect to the specific independent variable being examined. Typical of the presentation is:

$$\partial C/\partial U,\ \partial C/\partial CR,\ \partial C/\partial YP > 0 \qquad (5.4)$$

$$\partial C/\partial Y < 0 \qquad (5.5)$$

$$\partial C/\partial V \gtrless 0 \qquad (5.6)$$

These partial derivatives outline the predictions of the theory underlying the model. The calculus contains no explanations of **why** these predictions are as they are. That information would be obtained from a reading of the details of the theory. But we do see **what** the predictions are. Equation (or, more exactly, 'inequality') (5.4) specifies that there is direct variation predicted between C and U, CR, and YP; (5.5) predicts inverse variation between C and Y; and (5.6) predicts either inverse or direct variation between C and V. Both types of predicted variation show that the theory suggests that there are forces represented by the variables which could cause the result to have an inverse and direct effect. It is a very sophisticated way of saying 'I really don't know how V affects C'.

Once these hypotheses are presented, all that remains is to use all the available relevant information to test the predictions of the theory. The available information takes the form of a matrix of numbers. Each of the variables will have a series of observations and these numbers can be analysed using the tools of **regression analysis**. Because there are more than two variables in most analyses (one dependent and two or more independent variables), the technique is called **multiple regression analysis**. The dependent variable is called a **regressand** and the independent variables are called **regressors**. The dependent variable is 'regressed on' the independent variables.

This testing of the theory with data takes us across the bridge from mathematical economics to econometrics and with this move we will discover the primary difference between **economic theorising** and **econometrics**. Economic theories are usually presented as **exact** or **deterministic** relationships. There is no error – all relationships are 'perfect' as in equation (5.7).

$$Y = B_0 + B_1 X \qquad\qquad (5.7)$$

The graph of such a deterministic relationship is shown in Figure 5.1.

The error term

Econometrics, however, requires that a **disturbance** or **error term** be included in any relationship. We leave the realm of

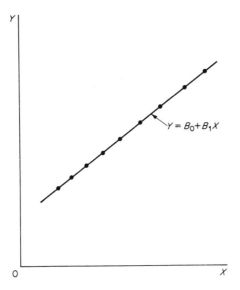

Figure 5.1

economics and enter that of econometrics with the inclusion of this error term. Equation (5.7) becomes

$$Y = B_0 + B_1 X + \epsilon \qquad (5.8)$$

where the Greek letter ϵ (epsilon) is the error or disturbance term. The graph which incorporates the idea of this error term no longer shows the data points falling neatly on a straight line but rather presents a scatter of points, some of which may fall on the line but most of which will not. Figure 5.2 illustrates such an inexact, statistical relationship.

Econometricians often refer to the error term as a **stochastic** error and the equation which incorporates it as the stochastic representation of the model. The word 'stokhos' means bull's eye in Greek and the difficulty of hitting the bull's eye every time is analogous to the inability to predict the exact value of a variable every time. But what are the causes of the errors?

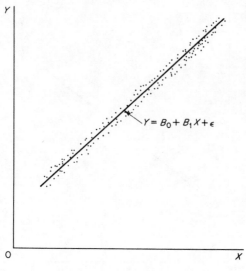

$$Y = B_0 + B_1 X + \epsilon$$

Figure 5.2

All predictions are subject to errors and these errors arise for many reasons. Some are called **specification errors** because the economic model being tested has left out (i.e. not 'specified') important explanatory variables. Others are called **measurement errors** because the variable could not be accurately measured. Some authors argue that the analysis of human behaviour will always yield some error simply because there is a random component to everyone's behaviour. An individual may respond in a certain way to a specific situation one day but behave quite differently when faced with that same situation another day, even if all the circumstances are the same. Because it is not possible to know all the potential sources of error, the actual size of the error is unknown. Therefore, the econometrician, for lack of a better alternative, makes some assumptions about the error term. These assumptions about the behaviour of the error term are a very important part of econometrics and a great deal of attention is paid to the testing of these assumptions whenever econometric research is undertaken.

Basic assumptions about the error term

The four most important assumptions made about the error term are as follows. First, the error terms are assumed to be **normally distributed**. A normal distribution is a popular 'bell-shaped' distribution which:

(1) Has only one peak ('unimodal').
(2) Is the same shape on both sides of that peak ('symmetric').
(3) Has the property that the probability of picking very large or very small values at random diminishes as these values move further away from their arithmetic mean.

Figure 5.3 illustrates a normal distribution.

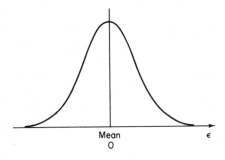

Mean
0

ε

Figure 5.3

The assumption of normality is quite strong but also quite popular and, unless there is a good reason to assume that the error terms are otherwise distributed, it is usually made. This is rationalised by arguing that there are many left out variables in any analysis, and, if the number left out is very large, their effects will 'average out' and give rise to a normally distributed error term. (This result is due to a statistical concept known as the Central Limit Theorem.)

The second assumption made about the error terms is that there is some sort of balancing between those that are positive and those that are negative resulting in the expectation that the value will be zero. Technically, this assumption refers to the **expected value** of the error terms – the expected value is zero. The mathematical notation uses something called the **expected value operator** and this assumption is conventionally written

$$E(\epsilon) = 0 \qquad\qquad (5.9)$$

where E is the expected value operator and there are n observations of each variable.

Assumption three concerns the *variance* (σ^2) of the error term. Variance is a measure of the dispersion of a series of numbers offering a very specific measure of the 'spread' of the data. It is calculated to provide some idea of 'average variation'. The disturbance term is usually assumed to have a variance which is both constant and finite. The technical term for a constant variance is **homoscedasticity**. The alternative, a non-constant variance, is called **heteroscedasticity.** The assumption of homoscedasticity means that the probability of finding an error term which is bigger than some specified value is the same when observations are taken at random. Further, the assumption means that all the things that generate the error term in the first place do not change over the data set being used. For example, if the ability to measure accurately the data being used in a study increases when more recent data is gathered, the error terms may get smaller when this more recent data is compared with older data. This would cause heteroscedasticity and is undesirable.

The last assumption usually made about the error terms is that they are independent of one another. The error term on observation 32 should not be related to the error on observation 31. The technical way of specifying this is to say that we assume **zero covariance** between any two error terms. If this assumption is violated there is said to exist a problem of **autocorrelation**. This may be caused by many things. For example, there may be an omitted variable which is generating some part of the disturbance term. To test for this it would be helpful to observe the error term but, unfortunately, we cannot. Instead, what we can see is a **residual**. The residual is similar to the error term in that both refer to deviations of actual data from the regression line. The difference is that the residual represents the distance of the data point from the **estimated** regression line whereas the disturbance or error term represents the distance of the data point from the **true** (unobservable) regression line. Therefore, in looking for the possible effect of an omitted variable, it is the residuals which are examined. If this omitted variable has a strong effect on a sequence of five or six observations, the observed residuals will appear to be correlated with one another. This problem often arises in time series data, especially if the data are daily or weekly. Sometimes, the omitted variable may have its own cyclical behaviour which is then transferred to the error terms. If there is autocorrelation, the interpretation of many of the results must be handled carefully.

These four assumptions are usually made about the data which are being used to test economic models – but how do we test these assumptions? There are some basic problems. First, it is not possible to observe **all** values of the variables and therefore calculate the **true** parameters. Because of this the true error terms are not observable. What is the econometrician to do? The conventional procedure is to assume that there is an unobservable world where the true values of all the desired parameters exist. But, because we cannot obtain all the data on all the variables we desire, we settle for what is available – a sample of observations on the variables in which we are interested. Using this sample and some method of estimation, the econometrician makes some guesses about the relationships between the variables as well as about the error terms. The residuals (which are measurable) can be calculated and analysed. These residuals can then be used in tests of the assumptions made on the error terms. The tests can sometimes show that the assumptions we are making are being violated, but they can never prove that the assumptions are correct. The best that can be done is to apply a set of data to a theory or model and test these assumptions as we are testing the theory. Before making any important conclusions about the results of the testing of our theory, we must be sure that the assumptions underlying the statistical test are not unrealistic.

In order to test a model, the econometrician attempts to estimate the relationships between variables. The method used is referred to as the **estimator** and the most popular estimator in applied research is called the **least squares estimator**.

The ordinary least squares estimator

A model of the relationship between one variable and a set of others can be specified as

$$Y=a+b_1X_1+b_2X_2+b_3X_3+\epsilon \tag{5.10}$$

where the b's are the parameters of the relationship. What the econometrician does is estimate the value of the b's – but there are virtually an infinite number of possible estimates of these parameters. What is wanted is the best estimate or, more precisely, the method which produces the best estimate. This method is usually referred to as the best **estimator**. A good estimator must fulfil certain requirements. Although there is a subjective element to what should be included in the list of requirements, and econometricians may argue about the length of the list, the most common requirements include mention of the following concepts: 'least squares', 'explained variation', 'best unbiased' and 'maximum likelihood'.

The idea associated with 'least squares' gives the method of ordinary least squares its name. Recall that residuals are the distances of the actual data points from the estimated data points (lying on the estimated regression line). The method of ordinary least squares minimises the sum of the squared value of these residuals. This is the most popular estimator used in applied research.

Related to the idea of minimising the sum of the squared deviations of data points from their estimates is maximising the 'explanatory power' of a model. The sum of the squared residuals can be thought of as a measure of the 'unexplained' variation in the dependent variable. The proportion of the variation in the dependent variable remaining is called the 'explained' variation and is represented by the **coefficient of**

multiple determination (R^2). It is defined as the proportion of the variation in the dependent variable 'explained' by the variation in the independent variables.

Minimising the sum of squared deviations is a desirable property of an estimator but it must not be at the expense of other properties. One which many econometricians consider of great importance is the 'best unbiased' quality. To see what econometricians mean by biasedness we need to introduce the idea of a sampling distribution and its associated properties.

Bias has a special, technical meaning in econometrics which has nothing to do with the concept of prejudice in common usage. The idea of bias is related to the expected value of the error term. Suppose we are trying to estimate the value of a parameter and we have at our disposal 100 samples of data – the model is estimated 100 times. Now, some method of estimation (the estimator) is used on each of these data sets. The result will be 100 estimates of some parameter, say *b*. If we looked at how these estimates are distributed we would notice that some are a little larger than others and that some are a little smaller. This is called a **sampling distribution** of the parameter, *b*. A great deal of econometrics is concerned with the properties of this sampling distribution. Some properties are seen as 'good' and others are seen as 'bad'. A plot of the sampling distribution can be seen in the **probability density function** shown in Figure 5.4. The probability density function is related to a plot of the number of times (the frequency) each estimate of the parameter ($\hat{b}$) is observed.

A very desirable property of the sampling distribution is that it has a mean value which is equal to the true value of

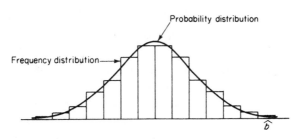

Figure 5.4

the parameter. Another name for the mean of the sampling distribution is the **expected value** of the distribution. An estimator is said to yield unbiased results if the expected value of the parameter is equal to the true value of the parameter. If the mean of the sampling distribution generated by some method of estimation is different from the true value of the parameter, the estimator is said to be biased and the amount of the bias is the difference between the mean of the estimated value of the parameter and the true value. **But be careful**. The econometrician does not say that **every** estimate of *b* is equal to the real value of *b*. Rather, the argument is that if a large number of samples were taken, the average value of the estimates would be correct. When this occurs, the econometrician says that the estimating method, the **estimator**, is unbiased. This is a desirable property. However, there is likely to be more than one unbiased estimator. Indeed, there are an infinite number of possibilities. Figure 5.5 shows three probability density functions which all have

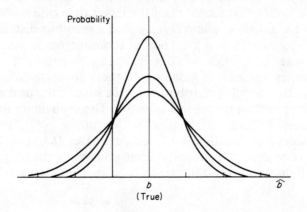

Figure 5.5

a mean (and therefore an expected value) equal to the true value of the parameter. But one distribution is more 'spread out' than the others, and one is the least 'spread out'. A popular econometric measure of such dispersion is called the **variance** (σ^2) of the distribution. If many unbiased estimators can be discovered, the one with the smallest variance of its sampling distribution is chosen. This is because the econometrician is more confident that the estimate based on a narrower sampling distribution is less likely to have wildly inaccurate, biased estimates than broader sampling distributions. The unbiased estimator that has the smallest variance is technically called the **best unbiased** or the **efficient** estimator.

Although this property is very desirable, it is usually very difficult to discover the variance of the sampling distribution. To keep the problem mathematically manageable, the estimator is assumed to be linear. If an estimator is the Best one possible; if it is also Linear and Unbiased, then the econometrician says that it is the Best Linear Unbiased Estimator or **BLUE**. (Econometricians like the **BLUE**s.)

Although the best linear unbiased estimator is one with many desirable properties, there is still another sought after characteristic – **consistency**. Consistency is usually discussed in the context of sample sizes. Sometimes an estimator does not satisfy the requirements of the econometrician when the sample size is small, but as the sample size gets larger and larger the requirements may be met. Such properties are known as large sample or **asymptotic** properties. An estimator is consistent if the estimated value of a parameter approaches the true value of the parameter as the sample gets larger and larger. Although the concepts of unbiasedness and consistency may seem similar they differ conceptually. Whereas unbiasedness refers to any sample of any size, consistency is a property of large samples only.

We see, then, that there are many criteria for a good estimator. The most popular estimator in applied research is the Ordinary Least Squares (**OLS**) estimator. Because of its popularity, it is usually the first estimator examined to see if it has the desirable properties. When it has these desirable properties, it is used – this is very often the case. But, unfortunately, sometimes the **OLS** estimator does not have enough of these properties. When this occurs an alternative estimator must be found.

The **OLS** estimator fulfils all the necessary requirements in what has come to be called the classical linear regression model. This model makes all the assumptions outlined earlier in this chapter plus a few more. For example, it assumes that the expected value of the error term is zero; it assumes that the error terms have a constant variance and are uncorrelated with each other; it assumes the dependent variable is a linear function of the independent variables plus a stochastic error term; it assumes that if different samples were gathered, the observations on the independent variables can be taken as fixed; and lastly, it assumes there are no linear relationships between independent variables (multicollinearity).

Once all the data have been gathered and loaded into a computer, the 'packaged' program will use an estimating method to produce estimates of the coefficients desired. The most popular estimator in these packages is the **OLS** estimator. The task of the researcher is to evaluate the results produced by this estimator. The results are usually output in the form of specified 'statistics'. Chapter 6 discusses the most important of these summary statistics. Understanding these summary statistics is the key to interpreting econometrics.

6

Important Statistics Generated by Most Regression Programs

The coefficient of multiple determination (R^2)

Probably the first thing a researcher looks at when viewing the results of a statistical test of some theory is the coefficient of multiple determination, or R^2. This statistic provides a measure of how good the theory is. By 'good' we mean how well the theory explains the facts. A good theory explains more than does a bad theory. But what do we mean by 'explains more'? The coefficient of multiple determination is the measure of 'more' and 'less'. It specifies how much the behaviour of something depends on something else. More exactly, the R^2 states the degree to which changes in a set of causal variables generate changes in some other variable. A formal statement of the meaning of the R^2 would be something like this:

The coefficient of multiple determination (R^2) describes the proportion of the variation in the dependent variable 'explained' by the variation in the independent variables.

This statistic therefore indicates how well the model performs – how well the explanatory variables 'explain' the dependent variable.

Consider a calculated value of 0.879 for the R^2. The correct interpretation of this decimal fraction is as follows:

An R^2 of 0.879 states that 87.9 per cent of the variation in the dependent variable is explained by the variation in the independent variables.

This interpretation provides a clue as to the range of values taken by the coefficient of multiple determination. If the equation specifying a model is very bad, it may explain very little, or, in the extreme, nothing at all. That is, zero per cent of the variation in the dependent variable is explained by the variation in the independent variables – reflected by a value of R^2 of 0.000. On the other hand, if the model is especially good, it may explain most, or in the (unlikely) extreme, all of the variation in the dependent variable – the R^2 takes a value of 1.000 – 100 per cent of the variation in the dependent variable is explained by the variation in the independent variables.

Most statistical analyses now carry the calculations of the R^2 one step further. They 'adjust it for degrees of freedom'. This is the solution to a problem which arose when it was discovered that the R^2 could be increased in value simply by adding more explanatory variables. It was possible to have it attain a value of 1.000 through the judicious selection of a great many independent variables. The adjustment procedure reduces the likelihood that increases in the value of the coefficient of multiple determination arise simply because the **number** of explanatory variables increased. In fact, the adjusted coefficient of multiple determination may actually **fall** if the additional explanatory power generated by an added variable is more than compensated for by the adjustment process. That is, the negative effect of the adjustment is larger than the positive effect of the added variable on the R^2.

A high R^2 will occur when the scatter of data points about an estimated regression line is small as in Figure 6.1. Deviations about the regression line will be large when the R^2 is low as in Figure 6.2.

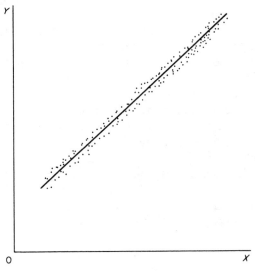

Figure 6.1

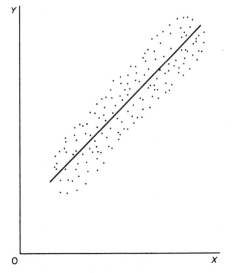

Figure 6.2

The R^2 is the square of the coefficient of multiple correlation. The word 'multiple' appears when there is more than one explanatory variable. If there is only one explanatory variable the analysis is called 'bivariate analysis' and the correlation coefficient is a 'simple' coefficient as opposed to a multiple coefficient.

More understanding of the R^2 can be attained from a discussion of the correlation coefficient. Correlation refers to the notion of 'co-movement'. Rather than looking at **explanatory power** (as the R^2 does) it simply measures the extent to which the variables move together.

If two variables are being examined we can plot the data points on a diagram to obtain a picture of the relationship. This diagram is called a **scatter diagram**. For example, suppose one variable is the price of some commodity and the other variable is the quantity of that commodity consumers wish to purchase at various prices. Placing the price on the vertical axis and the quantity on the horizontal axis a possible scatter diagram would look like that in Figure 6.3. Here, the quantity

Figure 6.3

demanded rises when the price falls and vice versa. A line passed through the data points in such a way that it is 'best fitting' would be a straight line with a downward (negative) slope. The simple correlation (simple because there are only two variables involved) would be negative because of the negative slope of the relationship. It would have a value somewhere between zero and minus one. It would not be zero because that would reflect no relationship, as in Figure 6.4, and it would not be minus one because that would be 'perfect correlation' wherein all the data points fell precisely on a line. The range of possible values of the coefficient of correlation is from -1.000 to $+1.000$, with the sign determined by the negative or positive slope of the estimated line.

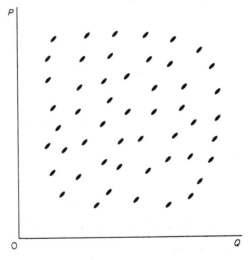

Figure 6.4

Because the best fitting line is a straight line the correlation is called **linear** correlation as opposed to **nonlinear** correlation which applies to curves. Most authors treat the word 'linear' as understood and refer to linear correlation as 'correlation' and apply the adjective nonlinear only when it applies. We shall follow this convention. Any discussion of correlation refers to the linear variety unless otherwise specified.

A different but related correlation possibility arises if we consider the relationship between the height and weight of a person. The scatter diagram for these variables is presented in Figure 6.5.

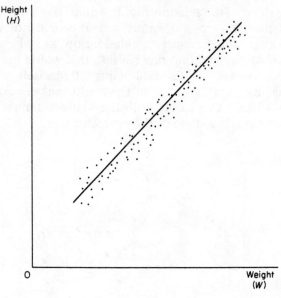

Figure 6.5

Although there are exceptions it seems that the taller a person is the heavier he or she may be. The scatter diagram shows an upward slope and the correlation coefficient will, reflecting this positive slope, have a positive value lying somewhere between zero and plus one. The closer the fit is to lying exactly along a line, the closer will be the correlation coefficient to one.

The 'eye-balling' of the data through the use of scatter diagrams is useful for gaining a qualitative idea of the relationship between two variables. Most researchers, however, prefer more exact notions of the relationship and therefore resort to more sophisticated measures wherein the exact value of the correlation coefficient is computed. Most packaged computer programs produce as part of their results these precise measures of correlation. The output of such 'software' (packaged programs) usually includes a summary table called a 'zero order correlation matrix' or simply a 'simple correlation table' which details the simple correlation coefficients between all the variables included in any regression equation. If more than two variables are correlated the coefficient name changes from simple correlation to multiple correlation. Multiple correlation refers to the extent to which three or more variables move together.

The qualifier 'multiple' is transferred from the idea of correlation to that of determination when regression analysis *per se* is considered. In regression analyses with two variables the simple correlation coefficient is transformed into the coefficient of determination. If three or more variables are included in the regression analysis the multiple correlation coefficient is transformed into the coefficient of multiple determination. The method by which the correlation coefficient 'becomes' the coefficient of determination is straightforward. **The coefficient of determination is the correlation coefficient squared.** Similarly, **the coefficient of multiple determination is the multiple correlation coefficient squared.** Hence a correlation coefficient of 0.8 would yield a coefficient of determination of $0.8 \times 0.8 = 0.64$. Because the coefficient of determination – be it simple or multiple – is the square of the correlation coefficient it cannot be negative. The square of a negative value for a correlation coefficient is a positive number. The result is that the coefficient of multiple determination always lies somewhere between zero and one.

Now, whereas a correlation coefficient near the absolute value of one (that is, near minus one or plus one) suggests a 'good fit', a coefficient of multiple determination approaching the value of one supports the **analytic validity** of the economic hypotheses inherent in the regression equation. But we must be careful how we interpret a low coefficient of multiple determination. A low coefficient must not be interpreted as indicating that the theory represented by the model is useless. The low coefficient merely states that only a small proportion of the variation in the dependent variable is explained by the independent variables. It may suggest that the model being tested is incomplete. That is, important variables are left out. But the relationships of the variables which are included in the model may provide very useful estimations of the reliability of the theorised economic relationships. For example, a model which attempted to explain why incomes differ among people may have as explanatory variables age and education. Suppose that the age and education variables were found to have a significant statistical relationship with incomes but that the R^2 was only 0.22. Only 22 per cent of the variation in incomes is explained by age and education signifying that the model is leaving out important explanatory variables. But the results of this test are not useless. The analysis reveals that there is a relationship between the variables included in the model. The R^2 could be improved by including more variables which have important effects on incomes, such as experience and family wealth. (These may not have been included initially because of the possible unavailability of such data.)

Given that the R^2 does not accept or reject specific hypothesised relationships between variables, the question turns to one of discerning when such relationships do or do not exist. This requires the interpretation of the partial regression coefficients.

Estimated partial regression coefficients

Estimated partial regression coefficients go by many names – regression coefficients, estimated coefficients, parameter estimates, point estimates, coefficient estimates and slope estimates to name the more common ones. (One author, for example, used three of these names for this statistic in a single paragraph of a technical article!) The partial regression coefficients are an extremely important part of any analysis. Their examination leads to the support or rejection of the hypotheses generated by economic theories. In these cases, relationships between **individual** variables are being examined.

Suppose we wish to discover the reasons for differences in the average earnings between industrial labour forces. The following linear equation could be used to test a theory of wage differentials by running the relevant data through a typical packaged computer program:

$$W = a + bEd + cX + dF + \epsilon \qquad (6.1)$$

where W, the dependent variable, is the average income of the members of some industrial labour force, Ed is the average number of years of schooling of the members of the labour force, X is the average number of years of work experience and F is the percentage of the labour force that is female. The a is the constant term, the letters b, c and d are the partial regression coefficients, and the ϵ is the stochastic error term. The partial regression coefficients can be thought of as 'weights' showing how movements in the independent variables Ed, X and F induce movements in W. More specifically, these weights **quantify** the relationships previously presented as **qualitative** by the theory.

Suppose the computer outputs the following results:

$$W = 21479.44 + 2341.29Ed + 3321.98X - 1042.67F + u$$
$$(6.2)$$

The partial regression coefficients specify the individual effect of each independent variable upon the dependent variable while holding the other variables constant. That is, the coefficient on the education variable quantifies the effect of education on income holding constant the amount of experience and the proportion of the labour force that is female. It is sometimes thought of as the **partial** effect of education on income – partial because the other variables which also contribute to explaining incomes are held constant.

A closer examination of these hypothetical results will clarify the meaning of these coefficients. The quantitative relationship between years of schooling and annual income is reported by the partial regression coefficient on Ed. It has a value of +2341.29. The plus sign indicates direct variation between Ed and W – an increase in Ed results in an increase in W and a decrease in Ed results in a decrease in W. But how much does *W* change for any given change in *Ed*? This is the information provided by the coefficient. Here is how the result is read. **A one unit change in the independent variable produces a change in the dependent variable equal to the value of the regression coefficient.** Hence a one unit change in the value of *Ed* **increases** the value of *W* by 2341.29 units. If education is measured in years completed and *W* is measured in dollars per year, we would say that a change of one year in the amount of education would change the annual income by $2341.29 in the same direction – an increase in education increases earnings and a decrease in education decreases earnings. So, if the average level of education of the labour force were to rise by one year we would expect earnings to rise by $2341.29.

The experience variable has the following effect, represented by the partial regression coefficient. A change in the number of years of experience by one year changes the average income in the same direction by $3321.98, *ceteris paribus* (no other variables changing). Positive signs on the coefficients indicate direct variation, hence the variables move in the same direction. The last variable, the percentage of the labour force that is female (*F*) has a negative sign indicating **inverse** variation. If the value of *F* rises the value of *W* falls; if the value of *F* falls the value of *W* rises. The coefficient indicates the magnitude of the change in *W* in response to a unit change in *F*. But what are the units of *F*? *F* is the percentage of the labour force that is female – it is a **percentage**. Measures expressed as percentages are very common in applied research and it is very important to interpret related coefficients very carefully. A one unit change in *F* is a change of one **percentage point**. Note that this differs from a 1 **per cent** change. If the **per cent** female rises from 10 per cent to 11 per cent the rise is **one percentage point**; but it is a 10 **per cent** rise (one percentage point in ten = 1/10th = 10%). The coefficent on *F* indicates that a **one percentage point** increase in the per cent female is associated with a decrease in the average income of the labour force of $1042.67. There is one qualification necessary – all these changes are most relevant to moves around the **mean** (arithmetic average) of the variables.

Accuracy of the partial regression coefficient

But how confident are we that this coefficient is accurate? To answer this question we introduce the concept of 'interval estimation'. The estimate of the partial regression coefficient is one of the parameters in which the econometrician is keenly interested. But we know that there is always an error associated with the estimations done in the realm of econometrics. A very common assumption made about the error terms is that they are normally distributed, which we have seen is part of the usual formulation of the classical normal linear regression model. The normal distribution permits the use of '*t*-tests' and '*F*-tests', which shall be discussed later.

In Chapter 5, it was pointed out that there is always a distribution of estimates of any parameter. Hence, no **one**, single estimate is necessarily the **true** value of the parameter. The set of estimates has a sampling distribution from which it is possible to obtain a probability distribution. The econometrician uses these distributions to construct measures of the reliability of the estimate. Such reliability is usually cast in terms of the 'level of significance' or 'confidence' associated with the estimated parameter. These levels vary from zero per cent to 100 per cent and it is conventional to refer to them in the following way. A **95 per cent level of confidence** is the same thing as a **5 per cent level of significance**; a 90 per cent level of confidence is the same as a 10 per cent level of significance; and so on. But what do the 'levels' in these cases refer to? To answer this we have to refer to the distribution of estimates of the parameter. These estimates are assumed to be distributed normally so that their distribution would look something like that in Figure 6.6.

The disturbances are measured along the horizontal axis and can be both positive and negative because the errors can arise from an estimate that is either larger or smaller than the true value of the coefficient. The height of the curve above the horizontal axis is directly related to the possibility of that specific disturbance being observed. Therefore, the higher the curve, the more likely that disturbance will occur, but the probability of any **single, specific** disturbance is quite small,

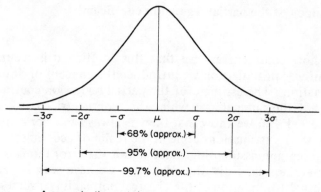

Areas under the normal curve

Figure 6.6

especially when there are many samples. So, rather than refer to the possibility or probability of a single result, we refer to the probability of observing values of the disturbance term appearing in some specified **range** along the horizontal axis. This probability is the **area under the curve** between the values of the disturbance term included in the specified range. The estimated coefficient is assumed to represent an unbiased estimate of the true coefficient and the deviations around this estimate are assumed to be normally distributed.

This assumption of normality is very important because it permits the use of the special characteristics of the normal distribution. Specifically, the probability of observing a value within a specified distance from the mean of the distribution – in this case the calculated regression coefficient – is related to the distance in each direction from that mean. If we chose a range of values which represent an equal distance from each side of the mean, the actual spread of the distribution is related to the probability of observing a value in the range of values. But if the spread affects probability, can we have the same probability applying to different spreads? The answer is yes, as long as the spreads are measured in terms of **standard deviations** (σ) about the mean. (A standard deviation is another statistical measure of the 'spread' of data around the mean.) In this way, one standard deviation in each direction from the mean has a different range of **actual** values for each normal distribution, depending on its spread, but it is **always** one standard deviation in each direction. A normal distribution with a relatively broad spread like that in Figure 6.7 would have a much larger range of values in a one standard deviation spread than would appear in one with a relatively narrow spread like that of Figure 6.8.

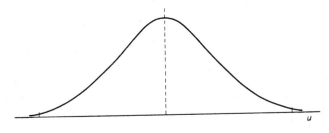

Figure 6.7

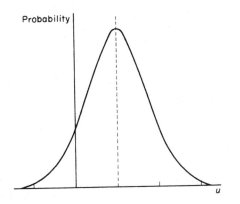

Figure 6.8

All normal distributions have the convenient quality that if we select a range of values that includes one standard deviation in each direction from the mean of the distribution, we will be able to make the same probability statement about the observed values. The probability of observing a value within a range one standard deviation in each direction from the mean is 0.6826 or about 68 per cent. If the range is enlarged to include two standard deviations the probability rises to 0.9544 or about 95 per cent. Three standard deviations in all directions includes almost all the observations and the probability of observing a value in this range is 0.9974. The favourite range size chosen by econometricians is the 95 per cent range. This is approximately two standard deviations in each direction from the mean. The exact number of deviations from the mean that would generate a probability of exactly 95 per cent is a little less than two deviations – it is precisely 1.96 standard deviations.

This can all be applied to the concept of interval estimation. The estimated partial regression coefficient represents exactly that – an **estimate**. There is an error term around that estimate. The error, we have seen, is assumed to be normally distributed so that we can make some statements about the distribution of estimates in different samples drawn from one population. Remember, we are trying to discover the **true** value of a parameter (in this case, the partial regression coefficient) when we do not have the entire population but only a sample drawn from that population. What the econometricians do is make a probability statement of this sort: 'the probability is 0.95 that the true value of the parameter is within the range bounded by the mean estimate minus 1.96 standard deviations and the mean estimate plus 1.96 deviations'. A convention is to call the standard deviation in this context the **standard error** or **se** of the coefficient.

This means that if we gathered many samples of the dependent variable and calculated partial regression coefficients over and over again, 95 per cent of all the estimates would fall in the range bounded by the mean plus or minus 1.96 standard errors. For example, if the mean value of the partial regression coefficients is 50 and the standard error is 5, then we would conclude that in a large number of samples, 95 per cent of the estimates would fall between approximately 40 and 60 – the mean minus two standard errors ($50 - 2 \times 5$) and the mean plus two standard errors ($50 + 2 \times 5$). (We have used 2 instead of the more exact 1.96 for mathematical ease.)

What we need is a simple and quick method of obtaining this sort of information about the spread of the errors around the estimated coefficient. Such information is captured in a test statistic referred to as the *t*-**statistic** and the test is usually called a *t*-**test**. This test statistic is used in making a very important decision concerning the estimated partial regression coefficient – is it zero or is it the estimated value? The possibility that it is zero is conventionally known as the 'null hypothesis'. The *t*-statistic helps us to decide whether to accept the null hypothesis (the estimated coefficient is zero) or to reject it (the estimated coefficient is not zero but is equal to the estimated value). Remember that the distribution of estimates is assumed to be normal. The probability that the true estimate lies within the range from the mean estimated value minus 1.96 standard errors to the mean estimated value plus 1.96 standard errors is 95 per cent. Replacing the 'mean estimated value' with the 'true coefficient', we say that if the true value of the coefficient is zero (the null hypothesis), the probability is 95 per cent that the estimated value will fall in the range from the mean minus 1.96 standard errors to the mean plus 1.96 standard errors. That is, if the true value is zero then there is a 95 per cent chance that the calculated coefficient will be near it. Symbolically,

$$-1.96se < \hat{B} < +1.96se$$

In terms of the absolute values of the deviations, we get

$$\hat{B} < 1.96se$$

Therefore, the probability is 95 per cent that the estimated partial regression coefficient lies within 1.96 standard deviations of the value of zero. But the other side of the statement suggests that there is a 5 per cent chance that the estimated partial regression coefficient is greater than 1.96 standard errors in each direction from zero. The equation

$$\hat{B} > 1.96se$$

can be rewritten

$$\hat{B}/se > 1.96$$

This ratio is often called a *t*-statistic (actually it has a distribution which is the same as a *t*-statistic) and it is the test statistic which is examined by econometricians and other researchers to test the reliability of their partial regression estimates.

If there is only a 5 per cent chance that the estimated partial regression is equal to zero, then there must be a 95 per cent chance that it is **not** equal to zero. If the calculated t-statistic is greater, in absolute value, than 1.96, then there is a 95 per cent probability that the partial regression coefficient is not equal to zero. That is, there is a 95 per cent chance that the true value of the coefficient is equal to its estimated value.

These calculations are approximate – the rule of thumb of about 1.96 is precisely that – a rule of thumb. To get the exact value of the t-statistic which serves as the reference value (the 'critical-t') in accepting or rejecting hypotheses, we need to reference a table illustrating the t-distribution. This is discussed at length in the following section.

The standard error of the coefficient

We have seen that the standard error of a regression co-efficient, in conjunction with that coefficient, helps to determine the reliability of the coefficient. More formally, the standard error is used to determine the **statistical significance** of the coefficient. The statistical significance refers to how confident we are that the estimated partial regression coefficient represents the true regression coefficient. The word 'significance' in econometric research is often used as an abbreviated form of the phrase 'statistically significantly different from zero'. The econometrician is attempting to discover if there is any relationship between a specified independent variable and the dependent variable. If there is a relationship the partial regression coefficient is interpreted as having the estimated value – a value different from zero.

This is where some confusion is possible. Very seldom do the computer results show coefficients as zero. Instead, they are usually printed as positive or negative numbers and can be quite large. How can there be any question that a coefficient with a printed value of 3321.98 may be no different from zero? On first contact, econometric analysis can be quite bewildering!

This is where the concept 'statistically different from zero' becomes important. Whether a coefficient is significantly different from zero in a statistical sense is determined by the relative sizes of the partial regression coefficient and its standard error. Equation (6.3) reproduces the partial regression coefficients of equation (6.2) and adds the standard errors of each coefficient.

$$W = 21479.44 + 2341.29Ed + 3321.98X - 1042.67F + u$$
$$\quad\;\;(800.31)\quad\;\;(400.19)\quad\;\;\;(6682.11)\quad\;\;\;(99.67) \qquad (6.3)$$

Whether a coefficient is viewed as being different from zero in a statistical sense is determined by the relative sizes of the coefficient and its standard error. Remember that the ratio of the partial regression coefficient to its standard error, b/se, follows the distribution of a *t*-statistic. For example, the *t*-statistic on the education variable, Ed, is

$$2341.29/450.19 = 5.20$$

Similar ratio calculations produce a *t*-statistic of 0.48 for the work experience variable, X, and -10.46 for F, the percentage female variable.

The first important point about these *t*-statistics is that **the sign is unimportant**. The sign of the *t*-statistic is determined by the sign on the regression coefficient because the standard error always has a positive sign. The **size** of the *t*-statistic is crucial; that is, its 'absolute value' is crucial. If the *t*-statistic is large enough, the partial regression coefficient is considered significantly different from zero in a statistical sense. If the *t*-statistic is too small, the partial regression coefficient is considered not significantly different from zero and the coefficient is read as a zero implying no relationship between the independent variable and the dependent variable in the equation as specified.

But how large is 'large enough' and how small is 'too small'? A *t*-statistic is large enough if it is bigger than a published critical value and too small if it is smaller than this critical value. The size of the critical value is determined by two things – the number of observations in the data set and the level of confidence desired. Examples of the number of observations are the number of years in a time-series study or the number of people in a cross-section study. The level of confidence refers to the likelihood of being correct. The critical value of the t-statistic varies inversely with the number of observations and directly with the level of confidence desired. The more observations in the data set being used, the lower the critical t-statistic for any given level of confidence; the higher the level of confidence desired, the higher the critical t-statistic for any given number of observations. Most research uses more than 15 observations and a popular 'cut-off' t-statistic occurs at the 95 per cent level. The critical t-statistic for 15 observations and a 95 per cent level of significance is shown in Table 6.1 as 2.13.

Although the number of observations is a very important determinant of the critical value of a t-statistic, the tables refer to something called 'degrees of freedom'. The number of degrees of freedom gets larger as the number of observations gets larger but it is always just less than the number of observations. It is calculated by considering the number of observations, the number of equations and the number of independent variables in the model. The procedure is as follows.

(1) Determine the number of observations in the data set (N).
(2) Count the number of **independent** variables in the equation (V) and add one to that number ($V + 1$) to take account of the equation representing the model. (Remember, the independent variables are those to the right of the equal sign.)
(3) Subtract the total in (2) from the number in (1). That is, symbolically:

$$\text{Degrees of freedom} = N - (V + 1) \tag{6.4}$$

This is the concept known as the degrees of freedom that is listed in the tables illustrating the critical t-statistics.

Table 6.1 *Student's distribution*

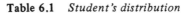

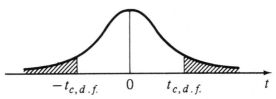

$-t_{c,d.f.}$ 0 $t_{c,d.f.}$ t

Degrees of freedom	Probability of a value greater in absolute value than the table entry					
	0.005	0.01	0.025	0.05	0.1	0.15
1	63.657	31.821	12.706	6.314	3.078	1.963
2	9.925	6.965	4.303	2.920	1.886	1.386
3	5.841	4.541	3.182	2.353	1.638	1.250
4	4.604	3.747	2.776	2.132	1.533	1.190
5	4.032	3.365	2.571	2.015	1.476	1.156
6	3.707	3.143	2.447	1.943	1.440	1.134
7	3.499	2.998	2.365	1.895	1.415	1.119
8	3.355	2.896	2.306	1.860	1.397	1.108
9	3.250	2.821	2.262	1.833	1.383	1.100
10	3.169	2.764	2.228	1.812	1.372	1.093
11	3.106	2.718	2.201	1.796	1.363	1.088
12	3.055	2.681	2.179	1.782	1.356	1.083
13	3.012	2.650	2.160	1.771	1.350	1.079
14	2.977	2.624	2.145	1.761	1.345	1.076
15	2.947	2.602	2.131	1.753	1.341	1.074
16	2.921	2.583	2.120	1.746	1.337	1.071
17	2.898	2.567	2.110	1.740	1.333	1.069
18	2.878	2.552	2.101	1.734	1.330	1.067
19	2.861	2.539	2.093	1.729	1.328	1.066
20	2.845	2.528	2.086	1.725	1.325	1.064
21	2.831	2.518	2.080	1.721	1.323	1.063
22	2.819	2.508	2.074	1.717	1.321	1.061
23	2.807	2.500	2.069	1.714	1.319	1.060
24	2.797	2.492	2.064	1.711	1.318	1.059
25	2.787	2.485	2.060	1.708	1.316	1.058
26	2.779	2.479	2.056	1.706	1.315	1.058
27	2.771	2.473	2.052	1.703	1.314	1.057
28	2.763	2.467	2.048	1.701	1.313	1.056
29	2.756	2.462	2.045	1.699	1.311	1.055
30	2.750	2.457	2.042	1.697	1.310	1.055
∞	2.576	2.326	1.960	1.645	1.282	1.036

Source: Reprinted from Table IV in Sir Ronald A. Fisher, *Statistical Methods for Research Workers*, 13th edition, Oliver & Boyd Ltd., Edinburgh, 1963, with the permission of the publisher and the late Sir Ronald Fisher's Literary Executor.

For purposes of illustration assume that there are 30 degrees of freedom for equation (6.3). From Table 6.1 we see that 30 degrees of freedom corresponds to a critical t-statistic ranging from 2.750 to 1.055 depending on the level of confidence desired. The figures at the top of each column indicate the level of confidence divided by two. Because each heading figure is only one-half the desired value, we double them to obtain the desired level of confidence. For example, doubling 0.005 gives 0.01 which is just another way of saying 1 per cent. Remember that researchers often refer to the level of 'confidence' in two ways: the '99' per cent level of confidence and the '1' per cent level of significance. Both of these mean the same thing.

Another example is shown in the third column with the heading '0.025'. Doubling this gives us 0.05 – the 5 per cent level of significance also known as the 95 per cent level of confidence. The value of the critical t-statistic – the **minimum** acceptable size of the ratio of the partial regression coefficient to its standard error – is 2.042 for 30 degrees of freedom.

Equation (6.3) presents both partial regression coefficients and their standard errors. The ratio of the coefficient to the standard error on the education variable is 2341.29/450.19 = 5.20. This means that the coefficient on the education variable is significant not only at the 95 per cent level but also at the 99 per cent level. (The critical t-statistic for a 99 per cent level is 2.750 for 30 degrees of freedom.)

The t-statistic on the experience variable is only 0.48 which is too low for any acceptable level of significance. The most common treatment of such a coefficient is to assume that the value is zero – there is no relationship between the experience variable and the level of earnings. That is, if experience changes by one year there is no effect on the level of earnings. Now, of course, there is no relationship in the model as specified but this does not mean that some other version of the model in some other mathematical form will not reveal a relationship. However, what most authors say in their discussion of statistically insignificant relationships (t-statistics too small) is simply that there is no evidence of a relationship from the data as applied to the model in the study.

The coefficient on the percentage female variable (F) is more than 10 times as big as its standard error (calculated t-statistic is -10.46) and indicates that a one unit change in the independent variable generates a change of $1042.67 in the level of income **in the opposite direction**. But care must be exercised in the interpretation of this relationship. The independent variable is the **percentage** of the labour force that is female. Therefore a one unit change in this variable is a one percentage **point** change. Remember that this is not the same as a 1 **per cent** change.

In the model of income we have presented there are two significant coefficients (those on ED and F) and one insignificant coefficient (on X). We would conclude that in the model as formulated, Ed and F determine income but that X does not.

The standard error of estimate

The standard error of estimate provides information about the **predictive power** of the model. (The R^2 provides information about the **explanatory** power of the model.) The standard error of estimate (SEE) is directly related to the stochastic error term u in equation (6.3). Packaged computer programs, in addition to generating information about the estimate of the error term (the residual), also provide a measure of the 'spread' of the data around the estimated regression line. This spread estimate is called the standard error of the estimate. It is usually examined with reference to the size of the mean of the dependent variable. The smaller the ratio of the SEE to the mean of the dependent, the greater is the predictive power of the model. If the value of the SEE in equation (6.3) is 1020.33 and the mean of the dependent is 21045.96 then the ratio, SEE/(Mean of Dependent), is 0.048 or approximately 0.05. The SEE goes into the mean about twenty times. This could be restated by saying that the SEE is about 5 per cent of the mean of the dependent variable. The **size** of the SEE on its own is of no importance; whether it is large or small in absolute terms does not matter. What matters is its size relative to the mean of the dependent. This is because of the manner in which the *SEE* is used. An *SEE* of 1020.33 is read as follows:

- 67 per cent of all the data points lie within a 'band' one standard error of estimate (1020.33) in each direction from the estimated equation;
- 95 per cent of the data points lie within a 'band' **TWO** *SEE*'s in each direction from the equation;
- 99 per cent of the data points lie within a 'band' **THREE** *SEE*'s in each direction from the equation.

Figure 6.9 illustrates these relationships.

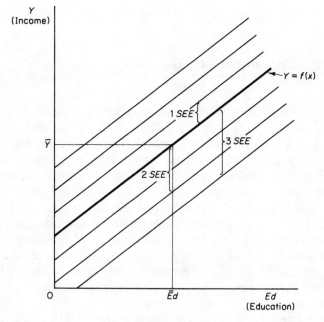

Figure 6.9

Remember that any regression line passes through the mean of all variables, dependent and independent. In the bi-variate case shown in Figure 6.9, the line passes through the mean of the dependent variable, $\overline{Y}$ (Income), and the mean of the independent variable, *Ed* (Education). The simplest view of the interpretation of the *SEE* visualises the error 'regions' as bounded by parallel straight lines as in Figure 6.9. Any movement in the independent variable will generate a predicted movement in the dependent variable. If the mean of the education variable is 11 years and it moves to 12 years we can estimate the anticipated change in the level of income. The expected change will have an error. From Figure 6.9, the suggestion is that the error will be related to the level of confidence desired. If we want a 95 per cent level of confidence (two *SEE*'s in each direction) the estimated income level will be 'plus or minus two *SEE*'s'. The estimate will therefore be plus or minus two times 1020.33 or 2040.66. The error region will range from two *SEE*'s less than the estimated income level to two *SEE*'s greater than the estimated value. Adding two standard errors of estimate to the mean income level is $2040.66 + $21045.96 = $23086.62. Subtracting two *SEE*'s from the mean gives us $21045.96 − $2040.66 = $19005.30. This gives the range of possible values (at a 95 per cent level of confidence) for the resulting income as from $19005.30 to $23086.62. Therefore, a change in education around its mean of 11 years will generate a change in income with an error of as much as 2 × $2040.66 = $4081.32! This is a rather large error and suggests that the results of the estimation are not useful for prediction. (For a 99 per cent level of confidence the potential error would be even larger.)

The analysis so far is based on the simplifying assumption that the error region is bounded by straight lines. But this is not true. Although such an assumption is often useful and, if estimates are around the means of all variables, not severely misleading, a more accurate representation of the error region is informative. Such an error region is shown in Figure 6.10.

Rather than being parallel straight lines the boundaries of the error region are actually curved. The size of the error grows as one moves away from the mean of the variables. The most accurate predictions are at the means of the variables. That is why many authors refer to 'movement of one unit **about the mean**'. It is also why predictions of dependent variable values made from independent variable values far from their means have a much greater probability of being incorrect.

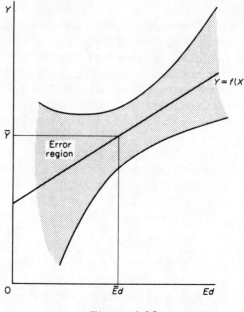

Figure 6.10

The F-statistic

Many computer software packages generate a summary statistic called an F-statistic. This statistic determines whether or not **all** the partial regression coefficients are equal to zero. In more formal terms it tests the 'null' hypothesis that

$$\beta_1 = \beta_2 = \beta_3 = \ldots = \beta_n = 0 \tag{6.5}$$

Some authors will state that this reduces to 'testing the significance of the coefficient of multiple determination (R^2)'. The method is fairly straightforward and very similar to the procedure used in examining t-statistics. The computer calculates an F-statistic which we then compare with a minimum (critical) F-statistic published in tabular form as in Table 6.2.

Reading the critical F-statistic is a little more difficult than reading the critical t-statistic. An F-statistic references two different degrees of freedom contexts. The first relates to the number of independent variables, n_1, and the second relates to the number of observations minus the number of independent variables minus one. The latter is the number of degrees of freedom as calculated in the previous discussion of the t-statistic. We will call it n_2. If the model we are examining has three independent variables, n_1, equals three. Further, if there are 27 observations on each variable, then n_2 equals $27 - 3 - 1 = 23$. Following the column for n_1 with a value of three down to the row where n_2 equals 23 we observe the critical value of the F-statistic, usually written as $F(3, 23)$. The table has two values, one in ordinary print and the other in darker, bolder type. These two values refer to the level of significance. Written at the top of the table is the level of significance corresponding to the two figures. In this table the two significance levels are 5 per cent and 1 per cent (or, equivalently, 95 per cent and 99 per cent confidence levels). The two figures for $F(3, 23)$ are 3.03 and 4.76. The lower figure refers to the lower level of significance and the higher figure to the higher significance level. If the computer calculated F-statistic is 6.92 we have confidence that **every** partial regression coefficient does not have a value of zero (although some may). In the jargon of statistics, we 'reject the null hypothesis that **every** coefficient is equal to zero'.

Should the calculated F-statistic have been 2.21 we would have accepted that null hypothesis and would have rejected the complete equation as specified because all partial regression coefficients are interpreted as being equal to zero. We would be back at square one and would try to build a new model explaining the dependent variable in whose behaviour we are interested.

The Durbin–Watson statistic: autocorrelation

One of the assumptions underlying a great deal of the regression analysis of time-series data is that the error terms in

Table 6.2 Critical values for the F distribution
5% (Roman type) and 1% (Bold face type) points for the distribution of F

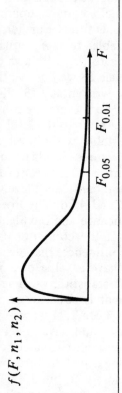

$f(F, n_1, n_2)$

n_1 degrees of freedom (for greater mean square)

n_2	1	2	3	4	5	6	7	8	9	10	11	12	14	16	20	24	30	40	50	75	100	200	500	∞	n_2
1	161 / **4,052**	200 / **4,999**	216 / **5,403**	225 / **5,623**	230 / **5,764**	234 / **5,859**	237 / **5,928**	239 / **5,981**	241 / **6,022**	242 / **6,056**	243 / **6,082**	244 / **6,106**	245 / **6,142**	246 / **6,169**	248 / **6,208**	249 / **6,234**	250 / **6,258**	251 / **6,286**	252 / **6,302**	253 / **6,323**	253 / **6,334**	254 / **6,352**	254 / **6,361**	254 / **6,366**	1
2	18.51 / **98.49**	19.00 / **99.00**	19.16 / **99.17**	19.25 / **99.25**	19.30 / **99.30**	19.33 / **99.33**	19.36 / **99.34**	19.37 / **99.36**	19.38 / **99.38**	19.39 / **99.40**	19.40 / **99.41**	19.41 / **99.42**	19.42 / **99.43**	19.43 / **99.44**	19.44 / **99.45**	19.45 / **99.46**	19.46 / **99.47**	19.47 / **99.48**	19.47 / **99.48**	19.48 / **99.49**	19.49 / **99.49**	19.49 / **99.49**	19.50 / **99.50**	19.50 / **99.50**	2
3	10.13 / **34.12**	9.55 / **30.82**	9.28 / **29.46**	9.12 / **28.71**	9.01 / **28.24**	8.94 / **27.91**	8.88 / **27.67**	8.84 / **27.49**	8.81 / **27.34**	8.78 / **27.23**	8.76 / **27.13**	8.74 / **27.05**	8.71 / **26.92**	8.69 / **26.83**	8.66 / **26.69**	8.64 / **26.60**	8.62 / **26.50**	8.60 / **26.41**	8.58 / **26.35**	8.57 / **26.27**	8.56 / **26.23**	8.54 / **26.18**	8.54 / **26.14**	8.53 / **26.12**	3
4	7.71 / **21.20**	6.94 / **18.00**	6.59 / **16.69**	6.39 / **15.98**	6.26 / **15.52**	6.16 / **15.21**	6.09 / **14.98**	6.04 / **14.80**	6.00 / **14.66**	5.96 / **14.54**	5.93 / **14.45**	5.91 / **14.37**	5.87 / **14.24**	5.84 / **14.15**	5.80 / **14.02**	5.77 / **13.93**	5.74 / **13.83**	5.71 / **13.74**	5.70 / **13.69**	5.68 / **13.61**	5.66 / **13.57**	5.65 / **13.52**	5.64 / **13.48**	5.63 / **13.46**	4
5	6.61 / **16.26**	5.79 / **13.27**	5.41 / **12.06**	5.19 / **11.39**	5.05 / **10.97**	4.95 / **10.67**	4.88 / **10.45**	4.82 / **10.27**	4.78 / **10.15**	4.74 / **10.05**	4.70 / **9.96**	4.68 / **9.89**	4.64 / **9.77**	4.60 / **9.68**	4.56 / **9.55**	4.53 / **9.47**	4.50 / **9.38**	4.46 / **9.29**	4.44 / **9.24**	4.42 / **9.17**	4.40 / **9.13**	4.38 / **9.07**	4.37 / **9.04**	4.36 / **9.02**	5
6	5.99 / **13.74**	5.14 / **10.92**	4.76 / **9.78**	4.53 / **9.15**	4.39 / **8.75**	4.28 / **8.47**	4.21 / **8.26**	4.15 / **8.10**	4.10 / **7.98**	4.06 / **7.87**	4.03 / **7.79**	4.00 / **7.72**	3.96 / **7.60**	3.92 / **7.52**	3.87 / **7.39**	3.84 / **7.31**	3.81 / **7.23**	3.77 / **7.14**	3.75 / **7.09**	3.72 / **7.02**	3.71 / **6.99**	3.69 / **6.94**	3.68 / **6.90**	3.67 / **6.88**	6
7	5.59 / **12.25**	4.74 / **9.55**	4.35 / **8.45**	4.12 / **7.85**	3.97 / **7.46**	3.87 / **7.19**	3.79 / **7.00**	3.73 / **6.84**	3.68 / **6.71**	3.63 / **6.62**	3.60 / **6.54**	3.57 / **6.47**	3.52 / **6.35**	3.49 / **6.27**	3.44 / **6.15**	3.41 / **6.07**	3.38 / **5.98**	3.34 / **5.90**	3.32 / **5.85**	3.29 / **5.78**	3.28 / **5.75**	3.25 / **5.70**	3.24 / **5.67**	3.23 / **5.65**	7
8	5.32 / **11.26**	4.46 / **8.65**	4.07 / **7.59**	3.84 / **7.01**	3.69 / **6.63**	3.58 / **6.37**	3.50 / **6.19**	3.44 / **6.03**	3.39 / **5.91**	3.34 / **5.82**	3.31 / **5.74**	3.28 / **5.67**	3.23 / **5.56**	3.20 / **5.48**	3.15 / **5.36**	3.12 / **5.28**	3.08 / **5.20**	3.05 / **5.11**	3.03 / **5.06**	3.00 / **5.00**	2.98 / **4.96**	2.96 / **4.91**	2.94 / **4.88**	2.93 / **4.86**	8
9	5.12 / **10.56**	4.26 / **8.02**	3.86 / **6.99**	3.63 / **6.42**	3.48 / **6.06**	3.37 / **5.80**	3.29 / **5.62**	3.23 / **5.47**	3.18 / **5.35**	3.13 / **5.26**	3.10 / **5.18**	3.07 / **5.11**	3.02 / **5.00**	2.98 / **4.92**	2.93 / **4.80**	2.90 / **4.73**	2.86 / **4.64**	2.82 / **4.56**	2.80 / **4.51**	2.77 / **4.45**	2.76 / **4.41**	2.73 / **4.36**	2.72 / **4.33**	2.71 / **4.31**	9
10	4.96 / **10.04**	4.10 / **7.56**	3.71 / **6.55**	3.48 / **5.99**	3.33 / **5.64**	3.22 / **5.39**	3.14 / **5.21**	3.07 / **5.06**	3.02 / **4.95**	2.97 / **4.85**	2.94 / **4.78**	2.91 / **4.71**	2.86 / **4.60**	2.82 / **4.52**	2.77 / **4.41**	2.74 / **4.33**	2.70 / **4.25**	2.67 / **4.17**	2.64 / **4.12**	2.61 / **4.05**	2.59 / **4.01**	2.56 / **3.96**	2.55 / **3.93**	2.54 / **3.91**	10
11	4.84 / **9.65**	3.98 / **7.20**	3.59 / **6.22**	3.36 / **5.67**	3.20 / **5.32**	3.09 / **5.07**	3.01 / **4.88**	2.95 / **4.74**	2.90 / **4.63**	2.86 / **4.54**	2.82 / **4.46**	2.79 / **4.40**	2.74 / **4.29**	2.70 / **4.21**	2.65 / **4.10**	2.61 / **4.02**	2.57 / **3.94**	2.53 / **3.86**	2.50 / **3.80**	2.47 / **3.74**	2.45 / **3.70**	2.42 / **3.66**	2.41 / **3.62**	2.40 / **3.60**	11
12	4.75 / **9.33**	3.88 / **6.93**	3.49 / **5.95**	3.26 / **5.41**	3.11 / **5.06**	3.00 / **4.82**	2.92 / **4.65**	2.85 / **4.50**	2.80 / **4.39**	2.76 / **4.30**	2.72 / **4.22**	2.69 / **4.16**	2.64 / **4.05**	2.60 / **3.98**	2.54 / **3.86**	2.50 / **3.78**	2.46 / **3.70**	2.42 / **3.61**	2.40 / **3.56**	2.36 / **3.49**	2.35 / **3.46**	2.32 / **3.41**	2.31 / **3.38**	2.30 / **3.36**	12
13	4.67 / **9.07**	3.80 / **6.70**	3.41 / **5.74**	3.18 / **5.20**	3.02 / **4.86**	2.92 / **4.62**	2.84 / **4.44**	2.77 / **4.30**	2.72 / **4.19**	2.67 / **4.10**	2.63 / **4.02**	2.60 / **3.96**	2.55 / **3.85**	2.51 / **3.78**	2.46 / **3.67**	2.42 / **3.59**	2.38 / **3.51**	2.34 / **3.42**	2.32 / **3.37**	2.28 / **3.30**	2.26 / **3.27**	2.24 / **3.21**	2.22 / **3.18**	2.21 / **3.16**	13

Column labels (printed along top and left margins): 14 15 16 17 18 19 20 21 22 23 24 25 26 27 28 29 30 32 34 36 38 40

Each cell is shown as the upper value / lower value.

df																								
14	2.13/3.00	2.14/3.02	2.16/3.06	2.19/3.11	2.21/3.14	2.24/3.21	2.27/3.26	2.31/3.34	2.35/3.43	2.39/3.51	2.44/3.62	2.48/3.70	2.53/3.80	2.56/3.86	2.60/3.94	2.65/4.03	2.70/4.14	2.77/4.28	2.85/4.46	2.96/4.69	3.11/5.03	3.34/5.56	3.74/6.51	4.60/8.86
15	2.07/2.87	2.08/2.89	2.10/2.92	2.12/2.97	2.15/3.00	2.18/3.07	2.21/3.12	2.25/3.20	2.29/3.29	2.33/3.36	2.39/3.48	2.43/3.56	2.48/3.67	2.51/3.73	2.55/3.80	2.59/3.89	2.64/4.00	2.70/4.14	2.79/4.32	2.90/4.56	3.06/4.89	3.29/5.42	3.68/6.36	4.54/8.68
16	2.01/2.75	2.02/2.77	2.04/2.80	2.07/2.86	2.09/2.89	2.13/2.96	2.16/3.01	2.20/3.10	2.24/3.18	2.28/3.25	2.33/3.37	2.37/3.45	2.42/3.55	2.45/3.61	2.49/3.69	2.54/3.78	2.59/3.89	2.66/4.03	2.74/4.20	2.85/4.44	3.01/4.77	3.24/5.29	3.63/6.23	4.49/8.53
17	1.96/2.65	1.97/2.67	1.99/2.70	2.02/2.76	2.04/2.79	2.08/2.86	2.11/2.92	2.15/3.00	2.19/3.08	2.23/3.16	2.29/3.27	2.33/3.35	2.38/3.45	2.41/3.52	2.45/3.59	2.50/3.68	2.55/3.79	2.62/3.93	2.70/4.10	2.81/4.34	2.96/4.67	3.20/5.18	3.59/6.11	4.45/8.40
18	1.92/2.57	1.93/2.59	1.95/2.62	1.98/2.68	2.00/2.71	2.04/2.78	2.07/2.83	2.11/2.91	2.15/3.00	2.19/3.07	2.25/3.19	2.29/3.27	2.34/3.37	2.37/3.44	2.41/3.51	2.46/3.60	2.51/3.71	2.58/3.85	2.66/4.01	2.77/4.25	2.93/4.58	3.16/5.09	3.55/6.01	4.41/8.28
19	1.88/2.49	1.90/2.51	1.91/2.54	1.94/2.60	1.96/2.63	2.00/2.71	2.02/2.76	2.07/2.84	2.11/2.92	2.15/3.00	2.21/3.12	2.26/3.19	2.31/3.30	2.34/3.36	2.38/3.43	2.43/3.52	2.48/3.63	2.55/3.77	2.63/3.94	2.74/4.17	2.90/4.50	3.13/5.01	3.52/5.93	4.38/8.18
20	1.84/2.42	1.85/2.44	1.87/2.47	1.90/2.53	1.92/2.56	1.96/2.63	1.99/2.69	2.04/2.77	2.08/2.86	2.12/2.94	2.18/3.05	2.23/3.13	2.28/3.23	2.31/3.30	2.35/3.37	2.40/3.45	2.45/3.56	2.52/3.71	2.60/3.87	2.71/4.10	2.87/4.43	3.10/4.94	3.49/5.85	4.35/8.10
21	1.81/2.36	1.82/2.38	1.84/2.42	1.87/2.47	1.89/2.51	1.93/2.58	1.96/2.63	2.00/2.72	2.05/2.80	2.09/2.88	2.15/2.99	2.20/3.07	2.25/3.17	2.28/3.24	2.32/3.31	2.37/3.40	2.42/3.51	2.49/3.65	2.57/3.81	2.68/4.04	2.84/4.37	3.07/4.87	3.47/5.78	4.32/8.02
22	1.78/2.31	1.80/2.33	1.81/2.37	1.84/2.42	1.87/2.46	1.91/2.53	1.93/2.58	1.98/2.67	2.03/2.75	2.07/2.83	2.13/2.94	2.18/3.02	2.23/3.12	2.26/3.18	2.30/3.26	2.35/3.35	2.40/3.46	2.47/3.59	2.55/3.76	2.66/3.99	2.82/4.31	3.05/4.82	3.44/5.72	4.30/7.94
23	1.76/2.26	1.77/2.28	1.79/2.32	1.82/2.37	1.84/2.41	1.89/2.48	1.91/2.53	1.96/2.62	2.00/2.70	2.04/2.78	2.10/2.89	2.14/2.97	2.20/3.07	2.24/3.14	2.28/3.21	2.32/3.30	2.37/3.41	2.45/3.54	2.53/3.71	2.64/3.94	2.80/4.26	3.03/4.76	3.42/5.66	4.28/7.88
24	1.73/2.21	1.74/2.23	1.76/2.27	1.80/2.33	1.82/2.36	1.86/2.44	1.89/2.49	1.94/2.58	1.98/2.66	2.02/2.74	2.09/2.85	2.13/2.93	2.18/3.03	2.22/3.09	2.26/3.17	2.30/3.25	2.36/3.36	2.43/3.50	2.51/3.67	2.62/3.90	2.78/4.22	3.01/4.72	3.40/5.61	4.26/7.82
25	1.71/2.17	1.72/2.19	1.74/2.23	1.77/2.29	1.80/2.32	1.84/2.40	1.87/2.45	1.92/2.54	1.96/2.62	2.00/2.70	2.06/2.81	2.11/2.89	2.16/2.99	2.20/3.05	2.24/3.13	2.28/3.21	2.34/3.32	2.41/3.46	2.49/3.63	2.60/3.86	2.76/4.18	2.99/4.68	3.38/5.57	4.24/7.77
26	1.69/2.13	1.70/2.15	1.72/2.19	1.76/2.25	1.78/2.28	1.82/2.36	1.85/2.41	1.90/2.50	1.95/2.58	1.99/2.66	2.05/2.77	2.10/2.86	2.15/2.96	2.19/3.02	2.22/3.09	2.27/3.18	2.32/3.29	2.39/3.42	2.47/3.59	2.59/3.82	2.74/4.14	2.98/4.64	3.37/5.53	4.22/7.72
27	1.67/2.10	1.68/2.12	1.71/2.16	1.74/2.21	1.76/2.25	1.80/2.33	1.84/2.38	1.88/2.47	1.93/2.55	1.97/2.63	2.03/2.74	2.08/2.83	2.13/2.93	2.16/2.98	2.21/3.06	2.25/3.14	2.30/3.26	2.37/3.39	2.46/3.56	2.57/3.79	2.73/4.11	2.96/4.60	3.35/5.49	4.21/7.68
28	1.65/2.06	1.67/2.09	1.69/2.13	1.72/2.18	1.75/2.22	1.78/2.30	1.81/2.35	1.87/2.44	1.91/2.52	1.96/2.60	2.02/2.71	2.06/2.80	2.12/2.90	2.15/2.95	2.19/3.03	2.24/3.11	2.29/3.23	2.36/3.36	2.44/3.53	2.56/3.76	2.71/4.07	2.95/4.57	3.34/5.45	4.20/7.64
29	1.64/2.03	1.65/2.06	1.68/2.10	1.71/2.15	1.73/2.19	1.77/2.27	1.80/2.32	1.85/2.41	1.90/2.49	1.94/2.57	2.00/2.68	2.05/2.77	2.10/2.87	2.14/2.92	2.18/3.00	2.22/3.08	2.28/3.20	2.35/3.33	2.43/3.50	2.54/3.73	2.70/4.04	2.93/4.54	3.33/5.42	4.18/7.60
30	1.62/2.01	1.64/2.03	1.66/2.07	1.69/2.13	1.72/2.16	1.76/2.24	1.79/2.29	1.84/2.38	1.89/2.47	1.92/2.55	1.99/2.66	2.04/2.74	2.09/2.84	2.12/2.90	2.16/2.98	2.21/3.06	2.27/3.17	2.34/3.30	2.42/3.47	2.53/3.70	2.69/4.02	2.92/4.51	3.32/5.39	4.17/7.56
32	1.59/1.96	1.61/1.98	1.64/2.02	1.67/2.08	1.69/2.12	1.74/2.20	1.76/2.25	1.82/2.34	1.86/2.42	1.91/2.50	1.97/2.62	2.02/2.70	2.07/2.80	2.10/2.86	2.14/2.94	2.19/3.01	2.25/3.12	2.32/3.25	2.40/3.43	2.51/3.66	2.67/3.97	2.90/4.46	3.30/5.34	4.15/7.50
34	1.57/1.91	1.59/1.94	1.61/1.98	1.64/2.04	1.67/2.08	1.71/2.15	1.74/2.21	1.80/2.30	1.84/2.38	1.89/2.47	1.95/2.58	2.00/2.66	2.05/2.76	2.08/2.82	2.12/2.89	2.17/2.97	2.23/3.08	2.30/3.21	2.38/3.38	2.49/3.61	2.65/3.93	2.88/4.42	3.28/5.29	4.13/7.44
36	1.55/1.87	1.56/1.90	1.59/1.94	1.62/2.00	1.65/2.04	1.69/2.12	1.71/2.17	1.78/2.26	1.82/2.35	1.87/2.43	1.93/2.54	1.98/2.62	2.03/2.72	2.06/2.78	2.10/2.86	2.15/2.94	2.21/3.05	2.28/3.18	2.36/3.35	2.48/3.58	2.63/3.89	2.86/4.38	3.26/5.25	4.11/7.39
38	1.53/1.84	1.54/1.86	1.57/1.90	1.60/1.97	1.62/2.00	1.67/2.09	1.69/2.14	1.76/2.22	1.80/2.32	1.85/2.40	1.92/2.51	1.96/2.59	2.02/2.69	2.05/2.75	2.09/2.82	2.14/2.91	2.19/3.02	2.26/3.15	2.35/3.32	2.46/3.54	2.62/3.86	2.85/4.34	3.25/5.21	4.10/7.35
40	1.51/1.81	1.53/1.84	1.55/1.88	1.59/1.94	1.61/1.97	1.66/2.11	1.69/2.11	1.74/2.20	1.79/2.29	1.84/2.37	1.90/2.49	1.95/2.56	2.00/2.66	2.04/2.73	2.07/2.80	2.12/2.88	2.17/2.99	2.25/3.12	2.34/3.29	2.45/3.51	2.61/3.83	2.84/4.31	3.23/5.18	4.08/7.31

Table 6.2 (cont.)

n_1 degrees of freedom (for greater mean square)

n_2	1	2	3	4	5	6	7	8	9	10	11	12	14	16	20	24	30	40	50	75	100	200	500	∞	n_2
42	4.07/7.27	3.22/5.15	2.83/4.29	2.59/3.80	2.44/3.49	2.32/3.26	2.24/3.10	2.17/2.96	2.11/2.86	2.06/2.77	2.02/2.70	1.99/2.64	1.94/2.54	1.89/2.46	1.82/2.35	1.78/2.26	1.73/2.17	1.68/2.08	1.64/2.02	1.60/1.94	1.57/1.91	1.54/1.85	1.51/1.80	1.49/1.78	42
44	4.06/7.24	3.21/5.12	2.82/4.26	2.58/3.78	2.43/3.46	2.31/3.24	2.23/3.07	2.16/2.94	2.10/2.84	2.05/2.75	2.01/2.68	1.98/2.62	1.92/2.52	1.88/2.44	1.81/2.32	1.76/2.24	1.72/2.15	1.66/2.06	1.63/2.00	1.58/1.92	1.56/1.88	1.52/1.82	1.50/1.78	1.48/1.75	44
46	4.05/7.21	3.20/5.10	2.81/4.24	2.57/3.76	2.42/3.44	2.30/3.22	2.22/3.05	2.14/2.92	2.09/2.82	2.04/2.73	2.00/2.66	1.97/2.60	1.91/2.50	1.87/2.42	1.80/2.30	1.75/2.22	1.71/2.13	1.65/2.04	1.62/1.98	1.57/1.90	1.54/1.86	1.51/1.80	1.48/1.76	1.46/1.72	46
48	4.04/7.19	3.19/5.08	2.80/4.22	2.56/3.74	2.41/3.42	2.30/3.20	2.21/3.04	2.14/2.90	2.08/2.80	2.03/2.71	1.99/2.64	1.96/2.58	1.90/2.48	1.86/2.40	1.79/2.28	1.74/2.20	1.70/2.11	1.64/2.02	1.61/1.96	1.56/1.88	1.53/1.84	1.50/1.78	1.47/1.73	1.45/1.70	48
50	4.03/7.17	3.18/5.06	2.79/4.20	2.56/3.72	2.40/3.41	2.29/3.18	2.20/3.02	2.13/2.88	2.07/2.78	2.02/2.70	1.98/2.62	1.95/2.56	1.90/2.46	1.85/2.39	1.78/2.26	1.74/2.18	1.69/2.10	1.63/2.00	1.60/1.94	1.55/1.86	1.52/1.82	1.48/1.76	1.46/1.71	1.44/1.68	50
55	4.02/7.12	3.17/5.01	2.78/4.16	2.54/3.68	2.38/3.37	2.27/3.15	2.18/2.98	2.11/2.85	2.05/2.75	2.00/2.66	1.97/2.59	1.93/2.53	1.88/2.43	1.83/2.35	1.76/2.23	1.72/2.15	1.67/2.06	1.61/1.96	1.58/1.90	1.52/1.82	1.50/1.78	1.46/1.71	1.43/1.66	1.41/1.64	55
60	4.00/7.08	3.15/4.98	2.76/4.13	2.52/3.65	2.37/3.34	2.25/3.12	2.17/2.95	2.10/2.82	2.04/2.72	1.99/2.63	1.95/2.56	1.92/2.50	1.86/2.40	1.81/2.32	1.75/2.20	1.70/2.12	1.65/2.03	1.59/1.93	1.56/1.87	1.50/1.79	1.48/1.74	1.44/1.68	1.41/1.63	1.39/1.60	60
65	3.99/7.04	3.14/4.95	2.75/4.10	2.51/3.62	2.36/3.31	2.24/3.09	2.15/2.93	2.08/2.79	2.02/2.70	1.98/2.61	1.94/2.54	1.90/2.47	1.85/2.37	1.80/2.30	1.73/2.18	1.68/2.09	1.63/2.00	1.57/1.90	1.54/1.84	1.49/1.76	1.46/1.71	1.42/1.64	1.39/1.60	1.37/1.56	65
70	3.98/7.01	3.13/4.92	2.74/4.08	2.50/3.60	2.35/3.29	2.23/3.07	2.14/2.91	2.07/2.77	2.01/2.67	1.97/2.59	1.93/2.51	1.89/2.45	1.84/2.35	1.79/2.28	1.72/2.15	1.67/2.07	1.60/1.98	1.56/1.88	1.53/1.82	1.47/1.74	1.45/1.69	1.40/1.62	1.37/1.56	1.35/1.53	70
80	3.96/6.96	3.11/4.88	2.72/4.04	2.48/3.56	2.33/3.25	2.21/3.04	2.12/2.87	2.05/2.74	1.99/2.64	1.95/2.55	1.91/2.48	1.88/2.41	1.82/2.32	1.77/2.24	1.70/2.11	1.65/2.03	1.60/1.94	1.54/1.84	1.51/1.78	1.45/1.70	1.42/1.65	1.38/1.57	1.35/1.52	1.32/1.49	80
100	3.94/6.90	3.09/4.82	2.70/3.98	2.46/3.51	2.30/3.20	2.19/2.99	2.10/2.82	2.03/2.69	1.97/2.59	1.92/2.51	1.88/2.43	1.85/2.36	1.79/2.26	1.75/2.19	1.68/2.06	1.63/1.98	1.57/1.89	1.51/1.79	1.48/1.73	1.42/1.64	1.39/1.59	1.34/1.51	1.30/1.46	1.28/1.43	100
125	3.92/6.84	3.07/4.78	2.68/3.94	2.44/3.47	2.29/3.17	2.17/2.95	2.08/2.79	2.01/2.65	1.95/2.56	1.90/2.47	1.86/2.40	1.83/2.33	1.77/2.23	1.72/2.15	1.65/2.03	1.60/1.94	1.55/1.85	1.49/1.75	1.45/1.68	1.39/1.59	1.36/1.54	1.31/1.46	1.27/1.40	1.25/1.37	125
150	3.91/6.81	3.06/4.75	2.67/3.91	2.43/3.44	2.27/3.14	2.16/2.92	2.07/2.76	2.00/2.62	1.94/2.53	1.89/2.44	1.85/2.37	1.82/2.30	1.76/2.20	1.71/2.12	1.64/2.00	1.59/1.91	1.54/1.83	1.47/1.72	1.44/1.66	1.37/1.56	1.34/1.51	1.29/1.43	1.25/1.37	1.22/1.33	150
200	3.89/6.76	3.04/4.71	2.65/3.88	2.41/3.41	2.26/3.11	2.14/2.90	2.05/2.73	1.98/2.60	1.92/2.50	1.87/2.41	1.83/2.34	1.80/2.28	1.74/2.17	1.69/2.09	1.62/1.97	1.57/1.88	1.52/1.79	1.45/1.69	1.42/1.62	1.35/1.53	1.32/1.48	1.26/1.39	1.22/1.33	1.19/1.28	200
400	3.86/6.70	3.02/4.66	2.62/3.83	2.39/3.36	2.23/3.06	2.12/2.85	2.03/2.69	1.96/2.55	1.90/2.46	1.85/2.37	1.81/2.29	1.78/2.23	1.72/2.12	1.67/2.04	1.60/1.92	1.54/1.84	1.49/1.74	1.42/1.64	1.38/1.57	1.32/1.47	1.28/1.42	1.22/1.32	1.16/1.24	1.13/1.19	400
1000	3.85/6.66	3.00/4.62	2.61/3.80	2.38/3.34	2.22/3.04	2.10/2.82	2.02/2.66	1.95/2.53	1.89/2.43	1.84/2.34	1.80/2.26	1.76/2.20	1.70/2.09	1.65/2.01	1.58/1.89	1.53/1.81	1.47/1.71	1.41/1.61	1.36/1.54	1.30/1.44	1.26/1.38	1.19/1.28	1.13/1.19	1.08/1.11	1000
∞	3.84/6.64	2.99/4.60	2.60/3.78	2.37/3.32	2.21/3.02	2.09/2.80	2.01/2.64	1.94/2.51	1.88/2.41	1.83/2.32	1.79/2.24	1.75/2.18	1.69/2.07	1.64/1.99	1.57/1.87	1.52/1.79	1.46/1.69	1.40/1.59	1.35/1.52	1.28/1.41	1.24/1.36	1.17/1.25	1.11/1.15	1.00/1.00	∞

Source: George W. Snedecor, *Statistical Methods*, Ames, Iowa: The Iowa State University Press, 5th edition, 1956, pp. 246–249. Copyright © 1956 by the Iowa State University Press: reprinted by permission. The function $F = e$ with exponent $2z$, is computed in part from Fisher's table VI(7). Additional entries are by interpolation, mostly graphical.

different observations of the variables are not related. But when this is not true and the error terms are correlated we have the problem of **autocorrelation**.

Autocorrelation is a violation of one of the assumptions of the classical model. It exists if the value of the disturbance term associated with one observation is correlated with the disturbance term of the adjacent observation. This occurs most frequently with time-series data. There are four possibilities:

(1)   A positive disturbance term in one period may be associated with a positive disturbance term in the next.

(2)   A negative disturbance term in period one may be associated with a negative disturbance in the next.

(3)   A positive disturbance term in one period is associated with a negative disturbance term in the next.

(4)   A negative disturbance term in one period is associated with a positive disturbance term in the next.

The first two exhibit what is called **positive autocorrelation** and the latter two illustrate **negative autocorrelation**. Figure 6.11 presents the two types of autocorrelation diagrammatically.

Figure 6.11(a) shows positive autocorrelation and Figure 6.11(b) shows negative autocorrelation.

Positive autocorrelation could arise when some 'shock' is applied to the system and the effects of the shock last for several periods. The system may react very sluggishly to externally generated shocks. These shocks are generated from outside the system as are the disturbance terms so a shock which causes the disturbance terms to be positive in period *t* may, because of an inertial force, also cause the error terms in subsequent periods to be positive. Similarly, a negative disturbance term in one period may cause negative disturbances in several subsequent periods. In both cases, the sign of the series of disturbances is the same so the autocorrelation is called 'positive'. Other circumstances may cause a positive and negative error term to alternate systematically thereby generating 'negative' autocorrelation.

The major problem with autocorrelation is that it may cause the researcher to accept a partial regression coefficient as being significantly different from zero when it is not and

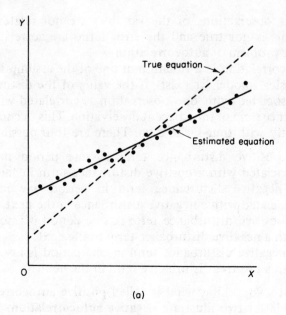

(a)

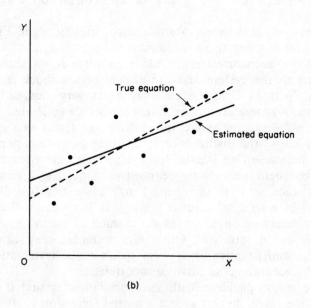

(b)

Figure 6.11

secondly it may cause acceptance of the null hypothesis that the partial regression coefficient is zero when it is different from zero. This arises because the '*t*-test' generates a *t*-statistic which is larger than the minimum acceptable value in the first instance and smaller than the critical value in the second. All of this occurs because the estimated standard error of the coefficient has a sampling distribution which causes the error variances of the estimated coefficients to be wrong.

Further, any given sample of autocorrelated data may generate over-estimates or under-estimates of the partial regression coefficients themselves. An over-estimate of the partial regression coefficient would result from the data set shown in Figure 6.12. The best-fitting regression line through the data points has a steeper slope than the 'true' relationship because the initial observation has a positive disturbance term and the autocorrelation caused subsequent disturbances to be positive until a negative one appeared. From that point the negative disturbances appeared for some time. The regression coefficient is larger than the true value and the coefficient on the constant term is too large.

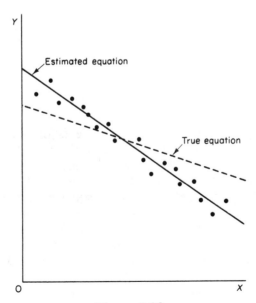

Figure 6.12

Of course, the initial observation of the data series may have had a large negative residual with the result that several subsequent observations would also have negative residuals until a positive one appeared. The positive residual would then begin a series of positive disturbances. In this case, the partial regression coefficient would indicate a slope that is steeper than the real slope and the intercept on the axis of the dependent variable would be too low as in Figure 6.13.

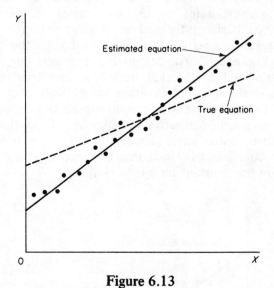

Figure 6.13

In many data sets these two effects of positive auto-correlation tend to even out so that the net effect on the partial regression coefficient is minimised. But there is an effect on the distribution of the error terms. The regression line fitted by the method of least squares (minimising the sum of the squares of the distances from the estimated line) will appear to have a better 'fit' than would the true relationship. This means it also has a smaller error variance.

One of the major causes of autocorrelation is an omitted variable or variables – possibly generating the 'shocks to the system'. Additionally, sometimes, the autocorrelation is caused by an incorrect functional form, such as applying a linear estimation to a curvilinear relationship as in Figure 6.14. But, whatever the cause, testing for autocorrelation is a central part of much empirical analysis.

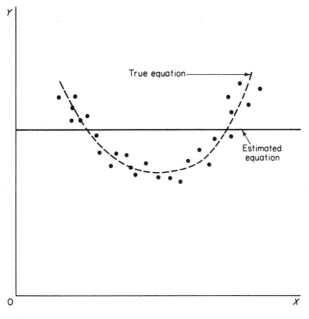

Figure 6.14

It is especially important to test for autocorrelation whenever time series data is analysed and the most frequent and popular test is that devised by James Durbin and G. S. Watson in 1951 which produces, not surprisingly, Durbin–Watson statistic, **D–W**. The Durbin–Watson test statistic is calculated in most packaged computer programs. The statistic can take a value from zero to four. The value which suggests that there is no autocorrelation is 2.00 and it is seen as a 'good' D–W statistic. Values greater or less than two are interpreted as indicating a potential 'autocorrelation problem'. The zero to four range of values of the D–W statistic is divisible into five zones. Two of them state that there is autocorrelation, one states there is no autocorrelation and the remaining two state 'we don't know'. Table 6.3 summarises the ranges.

Table 6.3   *Ranges of the Durbin–Watson statistic*

Value of d 0	d_L	d_U 2	$(4 - d_U)$	$(4 - d_L)$ 4
	Positive autocorrelation	Don't know	No autocorrelation	Don't know	Negative autocorrelation

What is most interesting about the D–W statistic is that there is a zone of uncertainty wherein we do not know whether or not the data illustrate an autocorrelation problem. Most other summary statistics generated by packaged computer programs have a 'yes–no' context. This black or white situation is altered with the inclusion of a grey zone for the D–W statistic.

There is a range around the ideal value of two where we say autocorrelation is not a problem. But just outside this zone the ability to answer yes or no to the autocorrelation problem is lost. This grey zone continues through values of the D–W until the zones indicating the existence of autocorrelation are entered. The boundaries of the five zones of the D–W statistic are presented in statistical tables in the same manner as t-statistics and F-statistics. Such boundary generating statistics are shown in Table 6.4.

The column heading n is the sample size and refers to the number of observations in the data set. (This is **not** the degrees of freedom concept discussed earlier.) The k in the table is the number of exogenous variables used in the equation. If there are 25 observations and three exogenous variables in the model being estimated the values of d which are relevant are $d_1 = 1.02$ and $d_u = 1.54$. This means that we can say that at a 95 per cent level of significance (the table refers only to this level of significance) one range of the D–W for which there is autocorrelation is zero to 1.02. Another zone of autocorrelation is given by the value of $(4 - d_1)$ to 4. This zone ranges from $(4 - 1.02) = 2.98$ to 4. The zone of no autocorrelation begins at a value of d_u which equals 1.54 and ends at $(4 - d_u)$ which equals $4 - 1.54$ or 2.46. Between 1.02 and 1.54 we do not know whether or not there is autocorrelation. This is also true for values of D–W between 2.46 and 2.98.

Table 6.4 *5 per cent significance points of d_l and d_u in two-tailed tests*

n	$k' = 1$		$k' = 2$		$k' = 3$		$k' = 4$		$k' = 5$	
	d_l	d_u	d_l	d_u	d_l	d_u	d_l	d_u	d_l	d_u
15	0.95	1.23	0.83	1.40	0.71	1.61	0.59	1.84	0.48	2.09
16	0.98	1.24	0.86	1.40	0.75	1.59	0.64	1.80	0.53	2.03
17	1.01	1.25	0.90	1.40	0.79	1.58	0.68	1.77	0.57	1.98
18	1.03	1.26	0.93	1.40	0.82	1.56	0.72	1.74	0.62	1.93
19	1.06	1.28	0.96	1.41	0.86	1.55	0.76	1.72	0.66	1.90
20	1.08	1.28	0.99	1.41	0.89	1.55	0.79	1.70	0.70	1.87
21	1.10	1.30	1.01	1.41	0.92	1.54	0.83	1.69	0.73	1.84
22	1.12	1.31	1.04	1.42	0.95	1.54	0.86	1.68	0.77	1.82
23	1.14	1.32	1.06	1.42	0.97	1.54	0.89	1.67	0.80	1.80
24	1.16	1.33	1.08	1.43	1.00	1.54	0.91	1.66	0.83	1.79
25	1.18	1.34	1.10	1.43	1.02	1.54	0.94	1.65	0.86	1.77
26	1.19	1.35	1.12	1.44	1.04	1.54	0.96	1.65	0.88	1.76
27	1.21	1.36	1.13	1.44	1.06	1.54	0.99	1.64	0.91	1.75
28	1.22	1.37	1.15	1.45	1.08	1.54	1.01	1.64	0.93	1.74
29	1.24	1.38	1.17	1.45	1.10	1.54	1.03	1.63	0.96	1.73
30	1.25	1.38	1.18	1.46	1.12	1.54	1.05	1.63	0.98	1.73
31	1.26	1.39	1.20	1.47	1.13	1.55	1.07	1.63	1.00	1.72
32	1.27	1.40	1.21	1.47	1.15	1.55	1.08	1.63	1.02	1.71
33	1.28	1.41	1.22	1.48	1.16	1.55	1.10	1.63	1.04	1.71
34	1.29	1.41	1.24	1.48	1.17	1.55	1.12	1.63	1.06	1.70
35	1.30	1.42	1.25	1.48	1.19	1.55	1.13	1.63	1.07	1.70
36	1.31	1.43	1.26	1.49	1.20	1.56	1.15	1.63	1.09	1.70
37	1.32	1.43	1.27	1.49	1.21	1.56	1.16	1.62	1.10	1.70
38	1.33	1.44	1.28	1.50	1.23	1.56	1.17	1.62	1.12	1.70
39	1.34	1.44	1.29	1.50	1.24	1.56	1.19	1.63	1.13	1.69
40	1.35	1.45	1.30	1.51	1.25	1.57	1.20	1.63	1.15	1.69
45	1.39	1.48	1.34	1.53	1.30	1.58	1.25	1.63	1.21	1.69
50	1.42	1.50	1.38	1.54	1.34	1.59	1.30	1.64	1.26	1.69
55	1.45	1.52	1.41	1.56	1.37	1.60	1.33	1.64	1.30	1.69
60	1.47	1.54	1.44	1.57	1.40	1.61	1.37	1.65	1.33	1.69
65	1.49	1.55	1.46	1.59	1.43	1.62	1.40	1.66	1.36	1.69
70	1.51	1.57	1.48	1.60	1.45	1.63	1.42	1.66	1.39	1.70
75	1.53	1.58	1.50	1.61	1.47	1.64	1.45	1.67	1.42	1.70
80	1.54	1.59	1.52	1.62	1.49	1.65	1.47	1.67	1.44	1.70
85	1.56	1.60	1.53	1.63	1.51	1.65	1.49	1.68	1.46	1.71
90	1.57	1.61	1.55	1.64	1.53	1.66	1.50	1.69	1.48	1.71
95	1.58	1.62	1.56	1.65	1.54	1.67	1.52	1.69	1.50	1.71
100	1.59	1.63	1.57	1.65	1.55	1.67	1.53	1.70	1.51	1.72

Source: J. Durbin and G. S. Watson, 'Testing for Serial Correlation in Least Squares Regression', *Biometrika*, vol. 38 (1951), pp. 159–77. Reprinted with the permission of the authors and the Trustees of Biometrika.

Once the computer has calculated the D–W statistic we can compare it with the tabulated values and determine the likelihood of autocorrelation. If there is autocorrelation one result is that the standard errors on each coefficient may be calculated as too small causing us to accept the partial regression coefficient at its calculated value when in fact it is statistically insignificant. That is, the calculated t-statistic is too high. It is too high not because the regression coefficient is too large but rather because its standard error is too small.

This concludes the discussion of the most important summary statistics generated by most computer software in the myriad of packaged programs available. But there are many problems associated with regression analysis. In addition to autocorrelation the most important of these go by the thoroughly frightening names of multicollinearity and heteroscedasticity.

7

Problems with Regression Analyses

Introduction

There are many problems which can occur with econometric analyses. The problems arise when the basic assumptions upon which all the statistical calculations are based are violated. Autocorrelation, discussed at some length in the last chapter in the context of the Durbin–Watson statistic, is one of the three most often discussed data problems. The other two are multicollinearity and heteroscedasticity. These are technical problems and are often called 'data' problems in that only certain data sets will cause them. They are frequently cast in the light of 'bad luck'.

Multicollinearity

Multicollinearity is the name statisticians give to the problem that arises when two or more of the independent variables in an equation are highly correlated. The prefix 'multi' is used whether two or twenty-two variables are correlated. If independent variables are collinear, they behave as if there is a linear relationship between them. The relationship could be positive so that when one goes up in value so does the other by a predictable amount; when one goes down by some amount, so does the other in a predictable way. The relationship could also be negative so that as one variable goes up in value, the other systematically goes down. The collinear variables move together – they act in many ways as a single variable. The result is that it becomes very difficult to separate out the individual effects of each collinear independent variable. An example helps to illustrate the problems arising from multicollinearity.

Suppose we are estimating an econometric model relating income (Y) to education (Ed), experience (X), age (A) and sex (S):

$$Y = \alpha + \beta_1 \ Ed + \beta_2 \ X + \beta_3 \ A + \beta_4 \ S + \epsilon \qquad (7.1)$$

where α is the constant term.

The data for these variables may reveal that the experience variable and the age variable are highly correlated. An increase in age almost always corresponds to an increase in experience and those individuals with less experience are almost always younger. The correlation coefficient can range from -1.00 to $+1.00$ with 0.00 indicating no correlation at all. Assume the correlation coefficient between X and A is 0.93. Such a 'high' correlation coefficient would indicate that the variables do, indeed, move together. If they are moving together to this extent, the separate effect of age on income is very difficult to ascertain because experience may be the variable actually causing the variation in income levels. The standard statistical techniques programmed into the computer as part of the conventional software allocates the explained portion of the variation in a more or less arbitrary fashion between the age and experience variables.

The effect of all this on the summary statistics described in Chapter 6 is of the utmost importance. Multicollinearity can have major effects on the estimated results. The most important direct result is the generation of unrealistically high standard errors on the partial regression coefficients. The abnormally high standard errors are sometimes sufficiently large to cause the calculated t-statistic to be smaller than the critical t-statistic. This results in the erroneous acceptance of the 'null' hypothesis that the partial regression coefficient is effectively zero. We may mistakenly interpret the results as showing no relationship between an independent variable and a dependent variable when in fact one exists.

A second problem arising from the existence of multicollinearity is exceptional sensitivity to the data set being used in the estimation. This makes it very difficult to replicate results with slightly different data sets on the same variables. As scientific research is based on the ability to replicate results this sort of difficulty is most undesirable. The partial regression coefficients estimated from one data set may be different from those estimated from another data set if multicollinearity is a problem with either.

A third problem arising from the existence of multicollinearity is that the results of the estimation depend greatly on the exact specification of the model being tested. An apparently minor change in the model being estimated that would normally have very small or even negligible effects on the parameter estimates will generate grossly different results when independent variables are collinear. Relatively minor changes in the specification of the model should not cause drastically different partial regression coefficients.

How do we check for the presence of multicollinearity given the output of packaged computer regression analyses? Most such software includes in the print-out a table of 'simple correlation coefficients'. A common form of such a table is presented in Table 7.1.

This table, often called a 'zero-order correlation matrix', specifies the correlation coefficient between every variable in the equation estimated. Both dependent and independent

Table 7.1   *Zero-order correlation matrix*

	Y	X	Ed	A	S
Y	1.000	0.894	−0.641	0.921	0.043
X	0.894	1.000	0.943	0.897	0.215
Ed	−0.641	0.943	1.000	0.024	−0.399
A	0.921	0.897	0.204	1.000	0.004
S	0.043	0.215	−0.399	0.004	1.000

variables are usually included in these tables although sometimes a blank column is placed between the dependent and
independent variables.

The first thing to notice is that only one-half of the table
has to be examined. This is because one-half of the table is a
mirror image of the other half. The line which divides the
halves is the diagonal of 'ones' running from the upper left
to the bottom right. These ones indicate the correlation
coefficient of every variable with itself is perfect – the value
is 1.000. This is fairly obvious and the only real use of such
information is to divide the table into two parts. The two
parts are images of each other in that the correlation between
X and Ed is numerically equal to the correlation coefficient
between Ed and X. So it does not matter whether we travel
down the X column to the Ed row and read the correlation
coefficient of 0.943 or whether we travel across the X row to
the Ed column and read 0.943. Hence, only the triangle
bounded by the variable column, the bottom of the table and
the diagonal of zeros need be consulted. (Alternatively, we
could consult the triangle bounded by the top row of variables
the right side of the table and the diagonal of zeros. Both
triangles include exactly the same information.

To detect multicollinearity we scan this table for 'high'
correlation coefficients. But what is a 'high' value? There is
no cut and dried answer to this question. Each author has his
or her own view about what constitutes a 'problem level' of
r, the correlation coefficient. A 'high' r for some authors is
anything above 0.500; for others it is above 0.800. (These
could be −0.500 and −0.800 – the negative sign only indicates

inverse association. Concern is expressed when the **absolute value** of the r is too high.) Although there is far from agreement on a 'cut-off' value of the simple correlation coefficient, r, there is some consensus on the use of a value around 0.600. Correlation coefficients less than this are 'OK' and those greater than this between independent variables reveal multicollinearity.

In Table 7.1 we ignore the first column as it presents the simple correlation coefficients between the **dependent** variable and independent variables. We are concerned only with correlation between **independent** variables when we are examining the results for multicollinearity. In fact, the only part of Table 7.1 in which we are immediately interested is shown in the dotted lines of Table 7.2 and then presented separately as Table 7.3. There appears to be correlation

Table 7.2 *Zero-order correlation matrix*

	Y	X	Ed	A	S
Y	1.000	0.894	−0.641	0.921	0.043
X	0.894	1.000	0.943	0.897	0.215
Ed	−0.641	0.943	1.000	0.024	−0.399
A	0.921	0.897	0.204	1.000	0.004
S	0.043	0.215	−0.399	0.004	1.000

Table 7.3 *Independent variable correlation matrix*

	X	Ed	A
Ed	0.943		
A	0.897	0.204	
S	0.215	−0.399	0.004

(sometimes called 'intercorrelation') between experience, X, and education, Ed ($r = 0.943$), and age, A ($r = 0.897$). Hence, the inclusion of these three variables in the equation at the same time will cause the estimation to suffer from the potential problems of multicollinearity. Although the probability is low, it would be possible in this situation to have all partial regression coefficients turn out to be statistically insignificant (low t-statistics) but to have a high coefficient of multiple determination (R^2). This paradoxical result would be interpreted as saying that the equation (or model) explains a great deal of the variation in the dependent variable while at the same time no individual independent variable explains anything at all!

It seems, then, that if independent variables are correlated we have problems. But what are the solutions? There are several possibilities. The first, and perhaps most obvious, is to get a different data set on the same variables that has no multicollinearity. This would be an ideal way to proceed if **more data were available**. Unfortunately, this is almost never the case. Very few researchers have a pool of data so vast that they can select some subset of it and test their theories on it. Most of the time all available data is used in the study under consideration – I have yet to hear a colleague complain that there is too much information available on the chosen research topic! Unlike many laboratory sciences a paucity of data is the norm in the social sciences. Therefore, although it would be nice to select a different data set on the same variables, this is usually an unrealistic solution to the problem. We must try another solution.

A second possible solution to the problem of multicollinearity which is often used is a sort of 'second-best' solution. In order to at least get a hint of the size of the effect of a problematic independent variable, one drops all collinear variables. In the example presented in Table 7.3, we would just estimate an equation with X and S and independent variables omitting Ed and A. This may give us a clue as to the effect of experience (X) on income (Y). Notice that **all** collinear variables are excluded, not just one of them. If we wanted to find the effect of education on income we would want to exclude experience as it is collinear with education. Now, this type of solution is extremely imperfect and provides only a rough and ready way around multicollinearity. Excluding collinear variables, although the most commonly practised method of avoiding multicollinearity, should not be done in a random fashion. The theoretical underpinnings of the estimated model should be consulted and followed in deciding which variables to leave out. The usual approach is to keep the **strongest** variable, with respect to the **economics** of the model, in the estimated equation.

One conclusion which may occur to the reader is that there is no real, genuine solution to the problem of multi-collinearity as it appears in econometric research. This is true. Where it occurs, patchwork solutions are the best that are usually put forward. As statistical research advances, perhaps a neat solution will arise, but until that happens, we are left with the approaches of the sort outlined above.

Heteroscedasticity

Heteroscedastcity is the formidable name for the problem that arises when the data violate the assumption that the disturbance terms all have the same variance. Of course, all the error terms are not of the same size in a data set. But, is there some systematic increase or decrease in the size of the error terms? (The variance of the error terms varies directly with the size of the error terms.) If the variance is constant, the condition is known as **homoscedasticity**; if it is not constant, it is called **heteroscedasticity**.

Figures 7.1 and 7.2 show some examples of heteroscedasticity and Figure 7.3 illustrates homoscedasticity.

In Figure 7.1 the errors seem to grow larger as X approaches some value of X (say X_1) and then diminish thereafter. This systematic relationship between the errors and the **size** of X violate the assumptions upon which the statistical calculations are based. This is heteroscedasticity. Figure 7.2 illustrates error terms that grow continuously as X grows; the errors vary directly with the size of X. Again, such a systematic relationship between the error terms and the size of the independent variable is seen as indicative of heteroscedasticity. In Figure 7.3 the errors do not seem to be related in any systematic way to the independent variable. The errors which occur at lower values of X appear no different in magnitude

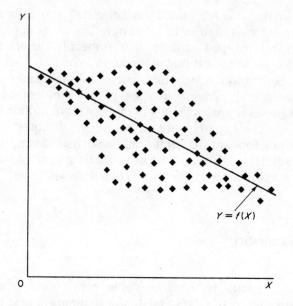

Figure 7.1

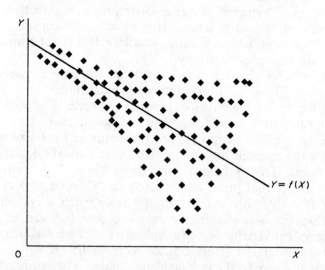

Figure 7.2

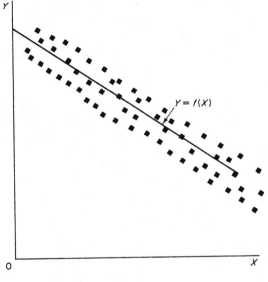

Figure 7.3

from those that appear at large values of X. This is a representation of homoscedasticity.

This 'eye-balling' technique – actually looking at the plot of the dependent variable against the independent variable – is usually the most efficient method of checking for the existence of heteroscedasticity.

Suppose that heteroscedasticity is found – what problems does this cause? The major effect is to cause the partial regression coefficients to be either too large or too small, depending on the exact pattern representing the heteroscedasticity. More precisely, the basic result of heteroscedasticity again concerns the variance of the parameter estimates with the potential result of making the incorrect decision concerning the reliability of the partial regression coefficients. Let us see why this may occur.

Heteroscedastic conditions mean that some variances are larger than others. If all variances are assumed to be of equal size and are given equal weight, as is done in ordinary least squares, then the large variances will be 'overweight' in their importance. This means that although the variances still have a mean of zero and are normally distributed, the ordinary least squares estimator is no longer the 'best' estimator. It is still linear and unbiased – we have not altered these assumptions, but it is not the best one. It is not the one with the **smallest** variance – it is not **BLUE** (Best Linear Unbiased Estimator).

The best one may be found by applying weights of some sort to the importance of the error terms with the intention of bringing the 'overweight' large variances back into line. If the appropriate weights are chosen, the new variances may be the same and we will satisfy the required assumption of homoscedasticity directly. Applying this procedure takes us from the realm of ordinary least squares in Generalised Least Squares, or **GLS**. The **GLS** estimator is considered to have a smaller variance than the **OLS** estimator and is therefore the 'best' one and hence is a **BLUE** (Unbiased Estimator). Another name for the 'best' one is the most 'efficient' one – we have satisfied the criterion of efficiency with the **GLS** estimator.

Although there are many methods which would take us from the **OLS** estimator to the **GLS** estimator, there is disagreement among econometricians as to when and even, if, the **GLS** estimator should be used. One of the problems that appears concerns the exact weighting that should be used. The precise transformation that should be applied is very difficult and sometimes impossible to find. Because of this many econometricians offer their own 'fix-it' kits in their writing but the consensus on the 'correct' way to handle the problem does not exist. Frequent advice given to the reader is to note that there is heteroscedasticity but not to act on it. That is, accept that the **OLS** is not 'efficient' in such a case but that any damage done is minor and, indeed, may be less than the damage done by the inappropriate application of **GLS**.

The problems discussed in this chapter and the last arise because of violations of the basic assumptions upon which the statistical testing takes place. Those assumptions apply specifically to the behaviour of the error term. Econometricians are continually attempting to find superior solutions to these problems as well as more refined ways of detecting them. It is important for the applied researcher to keep in touch with the latest developments in this area and to use the newest results wherever possible.

Index